The Street Smart Salesman

MAKING OPPORTUNITIES HAPPEN

Arthur Rogen

AVERY PUBLISHING GROUP INC.

Garden City Park, New York

Cover designers: Rudy Shur and Janine Eisner-Wall
In-house editor: Bonnie Freid
Typesetters: Coghill Typesetting, Richmond, Virginia

Library of Congress Cataloging-in-Publication Data

Rogen, Arthur
    The street smart salesman : making opportunities happen / Arthur
    Rogen.
        p. cm.
    Includes bibliographical references and index.
    ISBN 0-89529-487-7
    1. Selling. I. Title.
    HF5438.25.R63 1991
    658.8′5—dc20   91-19025
                                                                CIP

Printed in the United States of America

10 9 8 7 6 5 4 3 2 1

Contents

To the four jewels of my life. To my wife, Sally, who has always been the street smart driving force behind all my successes. To my daughters, Jennifer and Lisa, who will always be Daddy's little girls no matter how old they are. To my son, Eric, who has inspired me with his determination and courage to succeed.

Acknowledgments

My thanks go first to Martin Rogen, my father. He gave me the confidence to believe in myself and not to be afraid to achieve greatness. For that I will always be grateful.

My thanks also go to Eve Rogen, my mother. As I was growing up, she reinforced that my creativity and sense of humor were gifts, even when, at times, they got me into all sorts of mischief.

My thanks go to Abraham and Fanny Lefkowitz, my in-laws who have made me feel more like a son than a son-in-law.

My thanks go to Rose Lippman, my aunt. How lucky I have been to have someone in my corner like her. Her love has never been taken for granted.

My thanks go to Robert Sunshine, my oldest friend. They say that if you have one friend in life that you can count on, it is a gift. Rob is that friend. Thank God he made the wise decision to marry Jane, whom both Sally and I equally love.

My thanks go to Ira and Jo Sirota, who have spent many an hour acting as sounding boards for my various ventures. I shall never forgive them for moving to Las Vegas.

My thanks go to Irv Torbin, who has been a trusted friend and confidant during the past twenty years.

My thanks go to Scott and Debbie Gutterson, Ruth and

David Gantman, Laura and Gary Lefkowitz, Linda and Elliot Glasser, Roberta Kane, Toni and Fred Valenstein, Randy and Steve Galler, Gail and Danny Katz, and Bob Greenspan, who have been there for me through thick and thin.

My thanks go to Hal Markowitz, Iris Levine, Roger Gilbert, and Merrie Hollander, who gave me street smart insight into the original manuscript.

My thanks go to Eugene Dreyfuss, Douglas Szalai, Scott Gutterson, Stanley Kushner, and Roberta Kane, who were gracious enough to share their own street smart success secrets.

My thanks go to Bonnie Freid at Avery. Bonnie's special touch and careful attention to detail have been greatly appreciated.

My thanks go to all the street smart salesmen whom I have met through the years who have made this book possible. Special thanks go to Larry Wilson and Gene Lloyd, who early on taught me that being in sales is being in the greatest profession of all.

Lastly, my thanks go to Rudy Shur at Avery, who is most responsible for *The Street Smart Salesman*. Without Rudy's patience, insight and unfaltering confidence in my ability to write, I would never have been able to complete this book. His friendship is something that I will cherish forever.

Gender Bender

Yes, I know that the title says *The Street Smart Salesman*, and not *The Street Smart Salesperson*, but apparently the title *The Street Smart Salesperson* didn't quite make it in the mind of the publisher. The fact is, a "salesman" is as likely to be a female as a male. Also, when I do refer to sales folk, I use the masculine pronoun instead of the awkward "he or she" or "he/she". The decision to make the gender consistent was done in the interest of simplicity and clarity, not bias.

I believe the principles and tactics laid forth in this book have no gender boundaries. The freedom to pursue economic success is a birthright; we are limited only by our preconceived ideas of what we are capable of accomplishing, not by any words in a book.

Preface

Your first thought might be, "Why did he name this book *The Street Smart Salesman?*" Was I trying to be cute, using a clever catch-phrase as a gimmick to get your attention? No, this book is not meant to be cute. This book is not filled with MBA theories that sound good but don't cut it in the real world of competitive selling. This book was named *The Street Smart Salesman* because these are the people who make it happen. They are the achievers and winners in the world of sales. They make the *big bucks;* they are *successful!* If you want a piece of the action and desire to make the most of your selling opportunities, read this book. It is not meant to be cute; it is not gimmicky; it will become your sales bible. The knowledge in this book will help lead you to large commissions—it is street smart savvy!

I decided to write this book because too often during my twenty-two years in sales, I have observed salesmen who were not able to see all the wonderful opportunities that their profession could bring them. Many viewed sales as a dead-end job, and became progressively worse salesmen instead of better. The companies that I have consulted with often suffered because of this negative attitude.

This book is written for those who have to communicate the benefits of what they do, including just about everyone. Doc-

tors, lawyers, plumbers, gardeners, milkmen, etc., are all selling their services. What do you suppose it means when a
person says his doctor has an excellent bedside manner? It
means that the doctor has good communication skills; he
knows how to sell himself. When someone declares that his
attorney is the biggest and best in his field, what he is really
saying is that his attorney has communicated that feeling to
him. He has sold himself well. After all, from a technical point
of view, most of us are not in a position to judge the compe-
tency of the people that we choose to hire. *The Street Smart
Salesman* will make you the best in whatever you do.

If you are currently in sales, there is a chance that you
already know a street smart salesman. He's the guy who dis-
plays that cocky smile when your sales manager announces a
sales contest. You see, the street smart salesman knows the
contest is an incentive for the other salesmen to try to increase
their sales, whereas it is money in the bank for our street smart
salesman. He knows he's gonna win, and so does everybody
else around him. He hasn't lost a contest since he joined the
company. Before the first day is over for that contest, our man,
the street smart salesman, has his savings deposit slip filled
out. He is such a sure thing, Vegas wouldn't take odds against
him. Invariably, he sells any incentive trip he wins, choosing to
go to more exotic places.

You might not be aware of it, but you are in the greatest
business in the world, selling. Selling does not require you to
have a college education or to have been born on the right side
of the tracks. It's the great equalizer; it does not discriminate.
Many of the street smart salesmen I have known, including
yours truly, had nothing until they were fortunate enough to
see the fantastic opportunities a sales career could give them.
Street smart salesmen are the Rocky Balboas of selling. The
odds were against their ever becoming champions, yet they
beat all the odds. In my own case, when the bell rang at my first
sales job, I saw the opportunity and went for that brass ring.
Street smart salesmen don't roll with the punches; they lead
with their jabs and score knockouts. If you are not a champion,
start your training program now and read this book; gain street
smart savvy!

Many underachieving salesmen view street smart salesmen as arrogant con men. If they were con men, they could not produce year after year. What underachievers see as con is street smart creativity. Street smart salesmen are always looking for new ways of making money. They always see opportunity. For example, if our street smart salesman were driving in his Porsche convertible on a country road and suddenly plowed into Bessie the cow, destroying poor Bessie and his car, he would end up selling Bessie for hamburger patties and his car for parts, walking away with a mighty large profit. If you can imagine your having been on that country road, praying that your insurance would cover the damage, read this book. Get street smart!

As a result of their successes, street smart salesmen develop a confidence that their customers can feel. This confidence allows their clients to feel secure in doing business with them. Because of this feeling, street smart salesmen don't sell price. Selling price doesn't develop relationships. Selling price doesn't provide large commission checks needed to purchase all the great luxuries of life. Second money salesmen always sell price, especially when they are under pressure to meet their sales quotas for the month. Customers can sense in a flat second a salesman who is desperate, and they will squeeze you like a tube of empty toothpaste, leaving you little profit. If you sell price and are leaving lots of commissions on the table, read this book. Get street smart!

Street smart salesmen are rarely in the office. They know where the action is, and it's never at bull sessions at the water cooler. They persevere, they work hard, and they play hard. The harder they play, the more they enjoy their large commissions. Nothing will deter them.

Bugs Bunny is street smart. He doesn't allow anything, not even Elmer Fudd's bullets, to keep him from going after rabbit gold, carrots. Like the street smart rabbit he is, Bugs doesn't quit at the first signs of defeat. He reevaluates and tries again and again if need be.

If you are discouraged and have not accumulated many of the pleasurable items that you want, like a nice home, cars, etc. read this book. Throughout the book is information that will change the way you sell, and will change the way you feel about yourself and the kinds of goals that you set for yourself. I have written this book so that everyone will be able to benefit from the literally hundreds of tips and techniques that are offered. The book is broken down into two parts. Part One deals with the elements of the street smart salesman. These elements, such as motivation, discipline, and creativity, allow the street smart salesman to understand what he needs to develop himself so that he can reach the goals that he has set for himself. The second part of the book presents the skills of the street smart salesmen. In this section, you will be given street smart tactics. These tips will allow you to at least reach the next level of sales success. Many salesmen today simply rely on their personality to sell. That is not enough. To be successful, you have to know how to obtain clients, handle their objections, and close. This book has the tactics that work in your real world of sales. No matter what you sell, these techniques will make you the best at what you do. Get street smart. Don't become an Elmer Fudd salesman, always losing the order to a street smart salesman.

The best way that you can benefit from this book is to use it. Mark it up; make notes that will help you in your day-to-day selling. This book should become your sales bible. Don't skim through it and deposit it on your book shelf, never to be used again. Reread the chapters that zero in on the skills that you need to work on.

Scattered throughout the book are street smart success stories. These stories will give you an excellent idea of how other people have achieved greatness by becoming street smart salesmen. Read their stories. Hold them up as examples for yourself.

If you're still not convinced to read this book, answer this one question. How often have you walked out of a client's office shaking your head in disbelief and feeling frustrated because you could not close the deal? And I'm sure it has happened with customers whom you know deep down should have been sold. I'll tell you why you didn't make the sale—you haven't developed street smart savvy. If you are tired of coming in second and not making big bucks, take my advice and read this

book. Become a street smart salesman. Second money salesmen do not drive BMWs, and I mean the 700 series BMWs;
street smart salesmen do!

Like a lion walking the plains of Africa, street smart salesmen walk with a confidence that comes about only as a result of
enormous success. This book will give you an opportunity to
learn the secrets and techniques that make up a street smart
salesman's skills. For the past twenty-two years, I have used
these skills, and they have helped me to buy fantastic luxuries
that a poor boy from Brooklyn never believed were in his reach.
If you have what it takes to be a street smart salesman, this
book will help you reach for the good things in life. As I said in
the opening paragraph, this book is not meant to be cute. This
book is based on my experiences as an extremely successful
money-making street smart salesmen. Read it; gain the savvy!
The only thing you have to lose are your preconceived ideas of
what it takes to be successful.

Introduction

Street smart salesmen are the people who make things happen. They are the achievers and winners in the world of sales. They make the big bucks; they are successful! Street smart salesmen are confident, cocky, and tough. Nobody is going to take business away from their turf, nobody! Their biggest decision for the year is what color BMW they are going to get. Street smart salesmen are heads and shoulders above other salesmen.

Who are these other salesmen? Do these underachievers all sell, look, and talk the same way? Is the world of sales comprised only of super- and underachievers? No, that would be far too simplistic. As a sales trainer for the better part of twenty years, I have found that salesmen fall into four distinct categories. I will give you a description of each. I challenge you to put your ego in your back pocket and give some thought to the kind of salesman you are, and, more important, to the kind of salesman you want to be. It ain't easy, but it's street smart. Read on, gain the savvy!

In addition, I will tell you about the first street smart salesman I ever met. It was the most exciting and important day of my life. This allowed me to understand that I had the chance to become part of the greatest business in the world, sales. Once you gain the savvy, your opportunities are unlimited.

This book is based on my experiences as an extremely successful money-making street smart salesman. Let me do for you what that first street smart salesman did for me twenty-two years ago, make you successful. If you want to earn big commission checks, read this book.

The essence of street smart salesmen is that they hustle and use every skill that they can develop in order to close the sale. If we as salesmen do not write the order during the opportunity that we have with our prospect, you can bet that somebody else will surely follow and take what once was almost ours.

As a sales trainer as well as a consumer, I have been around literally thousands of salesmen and, as a result, have found that they fall into four different classifications.

First, there are the salesmen that I call the "order fakers." These salesmen will be able to sell only one out of ten prospects that they talk to. They wear shiny polyester clothing that enables you to see your own reflection as you reject their pleas to purchase. Their product knowledge is poor, their follow-up is nonexistent, and they find the need to talk incessantly about things in which you have absolutely no interest. After being subjected to them for ten or fifteen minutes, you find yourself contemplating a crime that could put you in jail for the rest of your natural life! By the way, you can spot these order fakers driving home in 1969 Dodge Darts, with depressed expressions on their faces. Woody Allen once said, "80 percent of success is showing up." In a sense, even when these order fakers show up, they aren't really there.

I call the second category of salesmen "order takers." Out of ten potential prospects, they will be able to convert two into actual sales. These people still gravitate to wearing polyester, but at least it is ironed. Scientifically, I don't believe there is a reason for their feet to appear abnormally large. They wear thin-ribbed socks that barely reach their ankles. A dirty brown tint shows on shoes, a result of their never having been polished, a nice touch if they were in construction.

The order takers have reasonably good product knowledge, and as a result should be able to bore you to death about minutiae within a fairly short period of time. As in the case of the order fakers, the order takers have to rely on customers who want their product so badly that they overlook their poor sales skills.

The order fakers as well as the order takers sell low price in order to close their sales.

Order takers drive Chevys and Fords, and seem to prefer colors such as putrid green and washed out yellow!

"Order makers" compose my third classification of salesmen. These people sell three out of ten clients. They are reasonably polished and have good product knowledge. They fall short of being charismatic, but to their credit they are not too offensive. They rely heavily on the "once-in-a-lifetime" close. This means that if you as a customer decide not to purchase at that very moment, you will never again be able to take advantage of that "once-in-a-lifetime" opportunity that they are proposing.

Their appearance is neat, colors of their clothes generally do not clash, and for the most part they look fairly professional. When they are feeling good about themselves, they have a tendency to wear every piece of jewelry that they own. Some develop "aurous syndrome," which is curvature of the neck caused by the excessive weight of their gold chains. They try to engage clients in conversation in order to discover customer needs; unfortunately, their approach is about as subtle as that of Inspector Clouseau, played by Peters Sellers in the *Pink Panther* movies.

Red Pontiac Bonnevilles appear to be their preference in cars. They order all sorts of gauges that not only inform them of when they will arrive at their intended destination based on their present speed, but, in addition, of how many times their kids are going to ask, "Are we there yet?" The car seats are covered in velour. Order makers rationalize that velour is superior to leather since it does not get hot in the summer. Deep down they know this is sour grapes, especially when they have the arduous task of cleaning up after one of their kids becomes car sick!

"Order shakers" round out our last category of salesmen. These shakers are the cream of the crop; they are street smart salesmen. They use their savvy to make big bucks. The street smart shakers are selfish; they do not like to share their customers with anybody. They want it all, and, for the most part, get it. Fakers, takers, and makers, like vultures scavenging through a carcass devoured by a hungry lion, pick up only bits and pieces of business left behind by the street smart salesmen. Like the cars they drive, these shakers are sleek, silky smooth, fast on their feet; and they understand that people buy for their own reasons, not the salesmen's; thus, they are able to maximize every sales situation that they encounter. Most superstar salesmen fall into this classification. I say most because there are situations in which a faker, taker, or maker happens to be in the right place at the right time, enabling him to get that one contract that affords him success far beyond his abilities. For the majority of the population, this is not a reality that we can count on.

The shakers can be extremely charming and are able to present themselves in a fascinating and electrifying manner. They are not afraid to be different or outrageous. They are constantly searching for new ways to improve themselves. They do not fear competiton; they welcome it. They do not sell price; they sell themselves. They are confident that they will survive and achieve greatness; they are street smart!

There is no question that I used a stretch of the imagination to embellish the negative characteristics of the faker, taker, and maker salesmen. What I did not exaggerate is the fact that most salesmen engaged in selling cannot sell. Neither did I exaggerate that street smart salesmen are the achievers of the world.

I ask you at this point what kind of salesman you want to be. Only you can answer this question. Fakers, takers, and makers have sold only one person well—themselves! They have sold themselves on the fact that they have done their very best. Some might say that they could have done better if they had just gotten a few breaks; but they didn't, and this is the way it has to be. Shakers, who are street smart salesmen, also sold themselves well, the difference being that they sold themselves on the fact that success is in their reach and that they control their own destiny. Rich or poor, they know it is a lot better to be rich.

Thank God, years ago I decided not to settle for mediocrity.

Settling is for losers, and I wanted no part of that; I was determined to be a winner. Let me tell you a little about myself and how I was persuaded never to accept second place.

Twenty-two years ago, my friend convinced me to attend a recruiting seminar for a company called United States Properties. They were looking for salesmen, and as part of their program they retained the services of Larry Wilson, future author of *One Minute Salesperson*, to speak on the advantages of entering the profession of sales. At the time, I was an elementary school teacher, clinging to the security of the position with rather low aspirations for myself. As Wilson strutted across the stage, I was immediately impressed with the confidence that emanated from him. Within seconds, he had all the people in the audience listening to his words as if he were a prophet, and in my case he was, for at that moment I was about to become a convert. I wanted more, and Larry Wilson convinced me that I could achieve it through the sales profession. I became a believer!

What impressed me most about Wilson's speech that day was his description of a salesman. Before I heard him speak, my perceptions were not too far removed from the salesman Willie Loman, the character in Arthur Miller's play *Death of a Salesman*. Some poor soul carrying a large beat-up sample case desperately trying to convince somone to purchase his wares in order to make ends meet for the week. This was far from an accurate description, according to Larry Wilson. According to Wilson, a professional salesman was an individual who had the opportunity to earn literally as much as he wanted. In addition, if he acquired the skills needed to become a professional salesman, he would not only gain riches but would have more security in his job than in any other occupation, since, as he put it, companies could not exist unless they employed salesmen who were able to sell their products or services. Though I had never thought of selling in that vein, I knew it had to be true. Logically, no matter how well a company manufactured a product or performed a service, if that company could not get the word out and get someone to say, "Yes, I would like one," the company could not survive.

Three hours or so later, I was determined to give up my

teaching position and enter the sales training program offered by United States Properties. After filling out the application, I practically ran home to tell my wife about my good fortune. The moment I arrived and began informing my wife about my career decision, my selling profession began. You see, my wife had not heard Larry Wilson speak. She did not believe I would have more security working as a commission salesman than an elementary school teacher, even though I was only making $5,600 a year at the time. To make matters worse, just as I was about to convince my wife, Sally, of the merits of my new venture, my parents dropped by our apartment. Upon hearing about my new career, my mother spoke to me as if I were about to commit the most heinous of acts, killing the two of them. My mother cried that if her college son left teaching, he would surely be murdering his father and her. My father took a more rational approach. He hoped that I had temporary insanity, and was sure I would regain my senses in the morning, especially after I realized how much money and sacrifice it had taken them to send me to college. I knew at that moment that if I were able to overcome the objections of the three of them, I had the makings to be the world's greatest salesman.

To be perfectly honest, I was able to convince only my wife that this was the right thing for me to do. My parents would not listen to anything I said, and again threatened to put their heads in the oven if I indeed left teaching. In addition, they informed me that if they survived the oven and I came to them for any sort of financial support, it would not be available. Nevertheless, with all this encouragement, I resigned from my teaching position that very week.

Looking back, it was the best decision I ever made. I became a salesman for United States Properties, rising from an entry-level position to that of vice president of marketing for their Eastern Marine Division in four years. My life was never the same. Within two years, I became their top in-home salesman, earning enough money to buy a magnificent home on the north shore of Long Island, thirty miles outside of New York City. In 1969, I made the prestigious "Million Dollar Club" and, as a result, the company held a dinner in my honor for 300-plus guests. Joe Paterno, the great coach of Penn State, was the master of ceremonies and presented me with a magnificent ring.

In 1973 I left United States Properties in order to start my own real estate development company. Six highly successful years later I sold my interests so that I could concentrate on my first love, teaching. Not teaching elementary school, but teaching salesmen who wanted to become successful in the greatest of all professions, sales. I am happy to report that I am doing just that, instructing salesmen on how they can take advantage of all the wonderful opportunities that are out there in sales. I have accomplished this by developing my own sales consulting firm. Over the years, I have worked with all types of industries, big and small, corporations or independently owned. What they have in common is a need to maximize their sales opportunities, and that is exactly what my programs and seminars have provided.

What this boils down to is that the street smart salesman has taken the principles of sales to a level much higher than most people engaged in selling are aware of. For twenty-two years, I have studied these principles and, more important, have put them into practical use, enabling me to close many an important deal.

This book is meant to give you both the understanding and the skills it takes to become street smart. I've divided this book into two parts: first, elements of the street smart salesman, such as motivation, discipline, and creativity; and second, the meat-and-potato sales tactics used by savvy street smart salesmen.

Look, I don't care where you come from, whether from the back bay of Boston or from the foothills of Tennessee. I know that if you put the knowledge you gain from reading this book into action, you will have the street smart savvy to be a winner! Go for it! It's worth it!

PART I
Elements of
the Street Smart Salesman

1
The Toys

Call me shallow, call me superficial, but make sure you call me rich! This statement may sound arrogant and obnoxious, but the truth of the matter is that money, in many instances, is the motivating factor for the street smart salesman. Of course there are other variables, but the key point is that these extremely successful street smart salesmen must be motivated by something. They know what they want, and they are motivated to take action to achieve because of the goals that they set for themselves. Street smart salesmen do not get up in the morning dreading to go to work. In fact, they cannot wait till the next day arrives, simply because they know it gives them another opportunity to get closer to their goals.

As a boy growing up in a one-bedroom apartment located in a poor melting-pot section of Brooklyn, New York, with my parents and two sisters, I used to dream about how fantastic it would be to have some of the luxuries I saw in the movies, like large homes, fancy cars, and snappy clothes. Being only eight years old, I probably would have considered it a luxury to have my own bedroom and not have to sleep on an old high-riser couch with my sister Linda, who constantly twisted and turned in her sleep and eventually stole all the blanket. One dreadful night, she accidentally flipped up the bar that lowered the bed, nearly decapitating me. Whoever said, "Those were the good old days," had to be rich! No way did he share his bed or stand on line to go to the bathroom in the morning.

Even as an eight-year-old boy, I was determined to succeed. My goal was to become rich enough to buy my mother a nice house where she would be able to garden all day. I had no idea back then that all my dreams would come true once I developed my street-smart skills.

You are never too young or old to start setting goals for yourself. Some people, like myself, start as young children dreaming about the good things in life. Others, like my Uncle Mickey, begin a second career in their late sixties. The key point is that people who achieve and live full and exciting lives are constantly setting goals for themselves no matter what their age. I guarantee that if you don't have goals motivating you to take action, you most likely are an underachiever, sleepwalking through life.

In this chapter, we will examine how the street smart salesman uses goals to help him reach greatness. Read this chapter, giving it great thought. It will help you develop and understand the proper way of establishing goals. Become shallow, become superficial, but, best of all, become rich!

All of us talk about goals in some fashion. Many would like to earn more money, drive a nicer car, have a larger home, etc. Unfortunately, most people merely talk about their goals, instead of working and planning to obtain them.

This holds true especially in the selling profession. We set quotas and commissions that we would like to earn, yet few of us make a conscious effort to work at these goals to achieve success. At times, goals are not even our own, but are set by others, making them even more meaningless. A sales manager often demands a certain amount of business, but in many cases this is a minimum standard to enable him to keep his job. In effect, the sales manager is reinforcing the notion that mediocrity is satisfactory.

There is nothing mediocre about street smart salesmen. These clever salesmen set high standards for themselves. Street smart salesmen do not sell themselves short settling for second best. They are not content just to go along meeting company sales quotas, which offers little more than job security. Street smart salesmen are always looking to increase their sales performance from month to month. The goals that the street smart salesmen set for themselves are considerably higher than any quotas that their company can possibly establish.

While I was a real estate salesman at United States Properties, some of my fellow salesmen used to question me as to why I pushed myself so hard. When I disclosed to them that my goal for the year was to make fifty-two sales, they thought I was absolutely crazy. In fact, some said that even if I somehow managed to accomplish this sales feat, I would surely pay the price by burning myself out. The company quota at the time was twenty sales a year.

I am happy to report that I did not even come close to burning myself out, even though I met my own sales quota for the year. The price I paid for setting higher standards for myself was being able to afford to buy a magnificent house and great cars, as well as other fantastic luxuries. Many of my colleagues who questioned my sanity became burnt out and disillusioned, leaving the field for greener pastures. If they had only set higher standards for themselves, they might have been able to take advantage of their opportunities and might have become neighbors of mine!

The street smart salesman realizes that only through hard work and preparation can he expect to reach the high standards that he sets for himself. Because the street smart salesman is so good at what he does, people do not believe that he works or prepares as hard as he does. They think that large commission checks come to the street smart salesman as if they were an act of God. This is nonsense. Street smart salesmen work very hard. They know if they do not prepare well they are wasting valuable opportunities for themselves.

Dr. Robert Shulber, author of *Move Ahead With Possibility Thinking,* states "that spectacular achievement is always preceded by unspectacular preparation." Preparation can be boring, mundane, and repetitive, but the street smart salesman is aware that there is no substitute for it. The wise salesman is always looking to learn more about his product or service. He wants to be prepared to answer any questions that might come up. In addition, the street smart salesman looks for new ways that the features of his product or service can best meet the needs of his client.

The street smart salesman frequently rehearses his presentation, seeing if there are any additional ways to fine-tune it. He knows that only through hard work, preparation, and scrutiny will he be able to remain on top of his presentation, sounding knowledgeable, fresh, and enthused.

On many occasions, salesmen will approach me and ask, "Arthur, why do you work so hard?" My reply to that question is always the same. I describe how one day, while walking through the streets of New York City, I came across a parked car that had a bumper sticker that read, "THE ONE WHO ACCUMULATES THE MOST TOYS BEFORE HE DIES, WINS!" I thought for a moment, and decided that here was one game that I absolutely had to win. It is a game that I take very seriously and work extremely hard at. Once I had begun to accumulate some of my "toys," I discovered that my desire to prepare, work, and win became stronger and stronger.

Most of us want the toys, but, when push comes to shove, are not willing to put the effort into obtaining them. Fakers and takers sell themselves on the idea that they are working hard simply because they arrive at work in the morning and leave in the evening. Fakers and takers, in many cases, do put in long hours, but they are nonproductive hours. Some even enjoy hanging out in the office. These salesmen are about as productive as the very chair that they sit on. Others convince themselves that they have found a short cut for success. Sadly for them, they realize too late in their career that this is never the case.

The story I am about to tell you is absolutely true and will further illustrate my point about how salesmen can easily fool themselves into believing that they are working as hard as they should.

When I was first married, my wife and I lived in an apartment house. Our next-door neighbor was a sunglass salesman named Steve. Whenever I happened to meet Steve in the building, he was either off to the golf course, tennis courts, or whatever other recreation he could find. I could never recall seeing him dressed for work. After a while, I questioned Steve about his work hours. Steve smiled and indicated that he had the perfect job. He told me how he did most of his business on the telephone, avoiding the inconvenience of making outside sales visits to his clients. He indicated that he had little difficulty making his sales quotas and was quite proud of the fact that he was able to fool his sales manager regarding how hard he was working. About five years ago, my wife and I ran into Steve and his wife at Macy's, a New York department store. Naturally, we asked each other how things were and what kind of work we were doing. Things had not changed much for Steve. He was still selling sunglasses and living in the same small apartment. He stated that he did not get the breaks over the years, declaring that all the promotions were going to the younger guys who kissed up to their managers.

There are a million Steves out there. Fooling the boss, wishing and hoping for success, but not willing to put in the hard work or preparation needed to achieve it.

If you want to become a street smart salesman earning the big bucks, you must work hard and study constantly at your profession. Unfortunately, most people don't want to work hard. The only way to achieve success without hard work and thorough preparation is through the lottery or an inheritance. For most of us this is not a reality. Abraham Lincoln said, "If I had nine hours to cut down a tree, I would spend six hours sharpening my axe." If you want to become street smart, start sharpening your axe. There are no short cuts. Without preparation and hard work, success will surely not follow.

Street smart salesmen write down their goals. Not only do they write down their goals, they write down how these goals will benefit them. The street smart salesman is keenly aware that this is the only way that his goals will become meaningful to him. In a sense, the street smart salesman has made a contract for success with himself, a contract he surely would not want to break.

The exercise of writing out his goals reinforces for the street smart salesman all the benefits that he will achieve once his goals have been met. This way, if he becomes discouraged, unmotivated, or sidetracked along the way, the street smart salesman can pull out his contract and clearly see the rewards that he will receive if he perseveres.

A few years ago I wanted to buy this classic MG sports car that I saw in the local dealership. I remember being a teenager, working as a caddy, and envying all the people whom I saw driving these cars. The color that I liked best was racing green, which happened to be the exact color that this dealership had. The MG was not very practical for a family of five, but was, nevertheless, a toy that I really wanted to have. I rationalized that if I could increase my sales by three a month, I could buy the car within a three month period of time, without spending money that was earmarked for other family projects.

I knew this would not be an easy task, and would require that I work even longer and harder. I also knew that there would be times when I would lose some motivation, especially when I would have to refuse my friends' invitations to play golf or tennis. But I wanted my MG. To insure that I would sustain my motivation, I wrote down my goal. Below is an example of how I typically write out my goals:

> *Goal.* During the months of June, July, and August, my goal is to increase my sales by three a month.
>
> *Benefits.* These additional sales will allow me to purchase that racing green color MG convertible that I saw at Competition Motors. Stay motivated and enthused. Remember, you already put a deposit down!

To be perfectly honest, I had to pull out my contract more than a few times that summer, especially when I was working while my friends were playing. But by the end of July, a month ahead of schedule, I accomplished my goal, and I felt like a teenager, as I motored around in my racing green color MG!

Underachievers, like the fakers, takers, and makers, never put down their goals in writing. If they did, they would discover that they are constantly breaking their own contracts. Because they do not write down their goals, the benefits of their goals become less important to them as they experience difficulty. As a result of this, there is no way that the fakers, takers, and makers are able to sustain their motivation over a long period of time. This is one of the reasons that they never achieve success—they frequently change their goals when they see the first signs of defeat.

Become successful—write down your goals. Like the street smart salesman, become accountable to yourself.

In addition to writing down his goals, the street smart salesman is aware that a key element to his success is to have specific and well-defined goals. In the goal that I described in the preceding paragraphs, I wrote down the specific color, racing green, as well as the specific model car, MG, that I wanted to buy, not being content to merely list "car" as my goal.

The street smart salesman's goals are so real and specific that he can clearly imagine he is in possession of them. For example, if a street smart salesman's goal is to own a sports car or boat, he is able to visualize his hair blowing in the wind as he goes speeding down the highway in his red Porsche convertible or sailing on the open ocean air in a Chris Craft yacht, cutting through the pounding waves. Notice that I didn't just say a car or a boat without naming the specific types. Street smart salesmen know specifically what they want. They want that red Porsche, they want that Chris Craft yacht that sleeps eight. They don't just list as a goal a car or a boat.

If a street smart salesman's goal is to earn a lot of money, the savvy salesman will write down the specific amount that he wants to earn. If your goals are not specific and well-defined, you will not be able to fully appreciate how they will benefit you once you achieve them. As a result, you will have trouble sustaining your motivation if things do not go as smoothly as you would like. Because of this, fakers, takers, and makers are like a boat without a sail, drifting from one goal to another, missing out on the success that they had hoped to achieve.

Define your goals so you can see vividly how they will benefit you. Set your sails and begin to steer your ship on the course of success!

Street smart salesmen do not have conflicting goals. Referring back to my goal of buying that MG, it would have been impossible for me to have set the goals as both increasing my sales production and, at the same time, cutting my working hours in half in order to pursue other interests.

People who have conflicting goals set themselves up for failure. It is not possible to eat junk food all day and to lose weight at the same time. When you are writing down your goals, make sure that they are not in conflict with each other. If they are, reevaluate them and choose the one that will offer you the most benefits.

Street smart salesmen set goals that are believable to them. They have the confidence that they can obtain these objectives. Underachievers become frustrated and discouraged in many cases because their goals are not goals, but are merely wishes. Deep down, the underachiever really does not believe he is capable of reaching these goals. He hopes for a miracle, like winning a lottery.

For example, I love to play golf, but it would be a totally unrealistic goal for myself to set my sights on scoring in the seventies even if the great Jack Nicklaus helped me putt. If I persisted in this unrealistic goal, I would soon become frustrated and lose the love for the game that I cherish so dearly.

Don't be a dreamer. Set goals that are realistic and believable to you. Take action; become street smart.

Street smart salesmen always set a time frame for their goals that is not so far in the future that the goals become meaningless. I recommend ninety-day goals. That does not mean we cannot plan for the entire year. What I am saying is, we should have check points every ninety days to see if we are on target and, if not, we should make the necessary adjustments to get back on track.

Be careful not to set up too many goals, whereby you are setting yourself up for failure, frustration, and procrastination. Fakers, takers, and makers have loads of goals. They want to be rich, they want to be thin, they want, they want, they want. . . . They have so many wants that they lose sight of their priorities. In addition, once one goal becomes a little difficult to achieve, they have a tendency to move to another objective that they believe is more obtainable. In the end, very little will be accomplished.

How do you reach your goals once they are set? First of all, like the street smart salesman, you must make a daily commitment to work as hard as you can.

Also, it is important to keep a positive attitude. Street smart salesmen think of themselves as winners.

At times, no matter how diligently you work, you will not always succeed in reaching your goals. The sensible street smart salesman understands that this is part of life, not just in sales, and tries to maintain a positive attitude towards himself as well as his work. The street smart salesman is aware that even though he did not reach an original objective, he can still have a positive learning experience. Willie Gayle, in his book *Seven Seconds to Success in Selling,* quotes Tryon Edwards, "Some of the best lessons we ever learn, we learn from our mistakes and failures. The error of the past is the wisdom and success of the future."

The street smart salesman makes it a habit to stay away from negative thoughts and from people who will discourage him from reaching his goals. Later on in the book I will discuss in greater detail the importance of having a positive attitude, as well as the negative effects that people can have on us.

Street smart salesmen know that in order to reach their goals they have to have excellent time management. They know that there are 86,400 seconds in a day, each one precious. Once they have passed, they can never be recaptured. Underachievers do not use their time wisely. Don't pretend that you are working when you are not. If you are behind your desk thinking about a round of golf, go play, but plan on how you are going to make up the time. If your mind is not on your work, utilize it on recreation, as long as it doesn't constantly take over your daily routine. Productive recreation can produce better results than nonproductive staring out the window.

Lastly, make things happen, do not wait and hope for good things to happen. George Bernard Shaw said, "The people who get on in this world are the people who get up and look for the circumstances they want, and, if they can't find them, make them." Street smart salesmen act quickly on their ideas and take advantage of opportunities when they present themselves. If your goals are written and believable, you can take hold of your life and make it happen.

It's easy to read about other people setting goals, but it's a lot harder to see exactly where you yourself stand in relationship to what you really want. The following questions are designed to help you come face to face with your desire to succeed as a salesman. Read these questions one at a time, and answer them either in your mind or on a sheet of paper.

1. Is your career going as planned?

2. What single factor has held you back from achieving more?

3. Do you see yourself as a winner?

4. If not, why not?

5. Do you set high standards for yourself?

6. If not, why not?

7. Are you working as hard as you can in your present job?

8. If not, why not?

9. Do you find your job boring?

10. Do you consider being a salesman a rewarding profession?

11. If you were given an opportunity to enter another field, would you choose to do so?

12. List the goals that you would like to obtain during the next twelve months.

13. List all the obstacles that you perceive you will encounter before you will be able to reach your goals.

14. List all the benefits that you will receive once these goals are met.

15. Do you see enough benefits coming to you to encourage your putting in the effort to reach these goals?

16. Write down a date when you will begin to commit to making your goals a reality.

17. Lastly, can you visualize having in your possession that first toy that you will buy yourself once you begin to achieve success?

Scary, isn't it? Maybe selling isn't for you. However, if your answers are in line with what you've just read in this chapter, you've just taken the first step towards becoming a street smart salesman!

2
The Fire

A fire burns way, way down inside the gut of the street smart salesman, which gives him the motivation to achieve. When he goes out to see a client he becomes Rambo in a business suit. The street smart salesman uses this motivation in order to achieve the high standards that he sets for himself. He is relentless; his fire keeps him working at a high, enthusiastic level, even during difficult times. This separates the street smart salesman from the fakers, takers, and makers, whose fire is quickly extinguished as they experience problems that send them back to the world of the nonachiever.

If you want the same type of fire that burns in the street smart salesman, you have to have certain elements in place. These elements are the things that fuel the fire. You not only have to understand them, but also to trust and believe in them; only then will you be on your way to becoming a street smart salesman.

What is motivation? Psychologists tell us it is an incentive for an individual to take action in some manner or form. Even though psychologists cannot agree on the mechanics of motivation, they do agree on the fact that each individual has particular needs. As soon as one need is satisfied, another need appears that motivates the individual to respond. Shelter, food, security (in the form of money), and recognition are some of the common needs shared by all.

Street smart salesmen share these common needs; the only difference is that because of their standards and aspirations, the needs they have are at a much higher level. For example, someone may find that earning $10,000 a year will satisfy his need for security, whereas the street smart salesman who has greater ambitions and wants would not feel secure unless he made $100,000 a year.

Everybody who has to work does so to satisfy the basic need of shelter, keeping a roof over his head. Many people, like the fakers, takers, and makers, would be happy enough living in a small apartment or a house so far from their job that they would have to spend half their life commuting. Street smart salesmen are also motivated to satisfy their basic need of shelter, although their idea of shelter may be a mansion!

A few years ago I had a consulting assignment with a company that manufactured stationery supplies. The owner of the company was in a quandary as to whether he should fire one of his salesmen. He explained that this salesman made an excellent appearance, was articulate, and seemed to have all the ability in the world, yet in the last two years was never more than a marginal producer for the company. The owner wanted me to see if I could determine why he performed so poorly.

After interviewing the salesman, it was easy to discover just what the problem was—he had little motivation.

The salesman told me he was living with his wife in the bottom apartment of a two-family house owned by his in-laws, *rent free!* Being mechanically inclined, he was proud of the fact that he was able to keep his 1977 Chevrolet, with 250,000 miles, going. *No car payment!* On top of this, he described his mother-in-law as the world's greatest cook, which he took advantage of at every meal. *No food bills!*

It is no wonder that this salesman did not perform; he had no incentives! Everybody was taking care of him. His aspirations were low and he had no difficulty meeting his needs. He was the original Freddie-the-Freeloader! I must be honest, this is more than enough to give a father like myself nightmares, since I have two daughters of my own.

Even though on the surface this salesman appeared to exhibit all the traits necessary for becoming a superstar, he lacked one important ingredient, motivation to succeed.

Street smart salesmen keep their motivation level high by having a positive attitude. This positive attitude turns them into fine-tuned fighting machines defeating any obstacles that get in their way. Their language is positive, using phrases such as, "Nothing can keep me from achieving success" and "I will reach my goals."

When a street smart salesman goes on a sales call, he can vividly picture himself making a sale. He sees himself effectively handling any objections that might come up. He sees himself getting the signed contract. Never does he see himself failing; street smart salesmen are always positive.

Underachievers of the world carry a negative attitude around as if it were part of their anatomy. They use language like, "I'm not sure I can do that," "How can they expect us to reach that sales goal?" As a result of this negative attitude, they can never visualize themselves as winners.

Street smart salesmen, not wanting to be negatively influenced by others, choose to stay away from people who do not have a positive attitude. They are aware that negative people have an almost subliminal affect on those around them. When a new incentive is announced, all the salesmen are at first excited and motivated to achieve. By the second week, one-third of the salesmen start to become negative. During the third week, these negative spreaders of doubt begin to adversely influence the next third of the sales force. Before the month is up, only the street smart salesmen, who had chosen to stay away from these negative people as if they had the plague, remain motivated to reach their goals.

It's a fact that you cannot tailor-make the circumstances in your life, but you can tailor-make the attitudes to fit those circumstances before they arise. Street smart salesmen do this by always trying to remain positive. The street smart salesman will not allow these negative people to eat away at his motivation as if he were a log infested with termites!

Street smart salesmen understand that once they identify a problem, it is their first step toward discovering a solution. These savvy salesmen know that the key to their success is to be solution-oriented and not problem-oriented. They are the eternal optimists in the selling profession. As a result of their positive and optimistic attitude, street smart salesmen see opportunity where others see doom and gloom. Problems are viewed as challenges that street smart salesmen work like the devil to overcome.

In 1973, the first gas crisis caused havoc in America. People had to wait on long lines hoping to get enough gas to get them through the week. Sadly, a few people were actually killed as a result of arguments that took place on line at gas stations.

Needless to say, it was not the best of times to be a real estate salesman selling recreational property to New Yorkers, ninety miles from their homes. The majority of my fellow salesmen virtually gave up trying to sell property. I viewed this as another challenge. There was no way that I would allow the gas shortage to keep me from making the living that I had become accustomed to.

Through hard and persuasive work, I was able to line up a few gas station owners who were willing to provide my customers with enough gas to get them up to see my property. At the time, I made arrangements to pay the owner twenty dollars for every one of my clients that he gave gas to. This was a small price to pay, especially when you consider that my average commission was $1,500.

If the customer bought the property, I gave him a card indicating that he was a member of the community upstate. As a result, he was able to get gas by paying the owner a five dollar premium when he filled up. My customers were tickled pink. I'm not so sure that they didn't just buy the property in order to get gas. Since the development had its own gas pumps, customers had no trouble going home.

As a result of my identifying a problem, and at the same time keeping a positive attitude, I was able to come up with a solution that turned a possible disaster into a money-making benefit to myself. It was not too long before the company observed my gas plan and made arrangements for the other salesmen's clients to get gas. I made thousands and thousands of dollars winning every sales incentive that the company offered during the gas crisis.

Become street smart, recognize all the fabulous opportunities that surround you. Winston Churchill, during World War II, implored the English people not to lose heart as a result of the merciless blitz the German air force had launched against England. He told his people that "an optimist sees a calamity as an opportunity, where as a pessimist sees an opportunity as a calamity." Take Churchill's advice, and become street smart!

Street smart salesmen keep their motivation high by not allowing failure to affect them.

Many salesmen, like the fakers, takers, and makers, fear failing so badly that it totally extinguishes their fire, causing them to give up on their effort to achieve. They get depressed and begin to feel sorry for themselves. They say things such as, "I can't catch a break," "I knew I shouldn't have tried that," and "Things never go right for me."

Because salesmen are so afraid to fail, they play it safe. Their motivation is so low that they only go after accounts that they feel secure in selling, in many cases avoiding the ones that offer the greatest monetary rewards. Street smart salesmen do not look for the easy way out. They are motivated to go where the money is, no matter how difficult it can get. The street smart salesmen will stop trying to sell these accounts only when they get a "yes."

My father had a friend Henry, who was a children's clothing salesman. Henry traveled throughout the northern part of New York. He was a hard-working salesman who frequently traveled hundreds of miles a day. Unfortunately, because Henry had a fear of failing, he worked harder and not smarter. Henry used to tell my dad and me how he needed patience like a saint when working with small mom-and-pop shops, constantly waiting for the owner to finish with a customer in order to show his samples.

When I questioned Henry as to why he would continue to sell only these small types of accounts, he mumbled that he didn't have the connections to get the bigger buyers to see his line. I knew this was bull. Fear of failure kept Henry from becoming a top producer. Henry took the route that he felt most secure with, small mom-and-pop stores where he wasn't intimidated. He was so afraid, he was not able to motivate himself to go after the real money-making accounts, preferring to continue to work harder for smaller commissions.

Street smart salesmen understand that the only way to avoid failure is to not try, and street smart salesmen will never give up trying. Street smart salesmen are so motivated that they never see failure as failure, but only as a learning experience. If they fail to reach their objective, street smart salesmen learn from their mistakes, and if anything, are more motivated to try again. Thomas Edison, in response to a question regarding the enormous amount of failure that he encountered while conducting his experiments, replied, "I did not fail a thousand times; I learned a thousand ways that it wouldn't work." Street smart salesmen are so motivated, they do not base their success on the number of times they have failed, but on the number of times that they have succeeded.

If a street smart salesman finds that he has a weakness, he works hard to overcome it, realizing that it is vital to his success in life and work to recognize his own weaknesses and limitations. Street smart salesmen are motivated to admit that they have a problem instead of burying their heads in the sand or blaming others for their shortcomings. Most nonachievers choose to run away from their flaws, lacking the motivation to try to overcome them.

When I first started out in sales, I was very weak when prospecting on the telephone. I found it boring and did not particularly enjoy being hung up on all day. Instead of running away from my problem, I was motivated enough to continually write out different telephone scripts, practicing on my wife, Sally, every night after work. In the beginning, I was so bad that my own wife hung up on me. Nevertheless, I was so motivated to succeed, I made myself into a dynamite telephone solicitor, never having to depend on others to supply me with leads.

Examine your strengths and weaknesses as a salesman. If you are to become street smart, you will have to work to overcome any deficiencies you might have.

The desire for recognition helps to keep the fire burning in the street smart salesman. He wants to be recognized for his good work by his fellow workers as well as by his family and friends. He rewards his own good work by purchasing luxury cars, expensive clothes, etc.

In 1972, I bought a fabulous midnight-blue Cadillac. The seats had the softest leather I have ever felt. Every conceivable gadget was elaborately spread across the dashboard. For me, owning a Cadillac meant that I had arrived!

I drove that Cadillac up and down, around and about my neighborhood, hoping that my neighbors would see me behind the wheel. At the time, I was doing quite well in business and I guess my ego wanted everybody to see just how well I was actually doing.

When I first showed the car to my dad, he looked at me with proud eyes swelling with tears and said, "Arthur, my bigshot son, I'm proud of you." Those words meant an awful lot to me.

It may seem shallow, but it is the truth. The recognition that I receive from my family, friends, and peers helps to give me the motivation needed to acquire additional material comforts associated with success.

In summary, the needs of street smart salesmen are no different than the needs of those who do not achieve great success. Both want security, shelter, and recognition. The difference between winners and losers is the level of motivation. The motivation of street smart salesmen to achieve is stronger. Street smart salesmen, because of their high motivation, are not afraid to fail and will create new challenges for themselves and go after the difficult sales. They do not blame others for their own mistakes or weaknesses. Their motivation is such that they set high standards for themselves and fully expect to reach them, no matter what it takes. They derive enormous gratification from the recognition that they receive from their peers.

The following questions are designed to help you look into the mirror and see exactly how brightly your own fire burns. Read these questions and answer them either in your mind or on a sheet of paper.

1. Do you have a specific well-defined goal that will motivate you to take immediate action?

2. If not, why not?

3. Do you generally have a positive attitude in relation to your work?

4. If not, why not?

5. Are the people around you, such as your wife, boss, friends, and fellow workers, positive or negative?

6. When something doesn't work out in your plans, what is your immediate reaction? What is your long-term reaction?

7. Do you avoid taking action on your ideas because you have a fear of failing?

8. What motivates you most: money, recognition, or security?

9. Where do you actually stand in relation to your own motivation?

10. If you are not where you would like to be, why not?

If you are not motivated to continue reading, selling is probably not for you. However, if your answers are in line with what you've just read in this chapter, you've taken the second step towards becoming a street smart salesman!

3
Keeping It Up

If Nintendo had a sales video game that required herculean effort to win, they would be wise to name it *the street smart salesman—sales warrior!* For the street smart salesman is the ultimate sales warrior, constantly battling enemies such as rejection, frustration, objections, and discouragement in order to come out on top and win the war of the *big bucks!*

If you are not a successful sales *soldier of fortune,* you must learn how to develop the single most important element of the successful street smart salesman, which is the perseverance necessary to sustain his motivation in reaching goals. Having the ability to persevere during the most trying times is the driving force that allows the street smart salesman to remain focused on what he wants to achieve. Only with that quality, will you be on your way to becoming a street smart salesman.

Most people confuse perseverance with motivation. It is not the same. They are worlds apart. The majority of underachievers can be very motivated but still fall far short of their goals. If they do not have the ability to keep it up when they see the first signs of defeat, they can never reach their objectives, no matter how bright or creative they happen to be.

President Calvin Coolidge once stated, "Press on: Nothing in the world can take the place of perseverance. Talent will not; nothing is more common than unsuccessful men with talent.

Genius will not; the world is full of educated derelicts. Persistence and determination are omnipotent." Street smart salesmen have the ability to press on.

Typical of the underachiever, his initial enthusiasm, which gives him the motivation to take action, disappears as he experiences the first signs of difficulty. Unlike the fakers, takers, and makers, the street smart salesman has a fifth gear that kicks in once his initial enthusiasm leaves, giving the street smart salesman the necessary perseverance to reach his goals.

Throughout my career as a sales trainer, I have come across many, many supposedly motivated salesmen who never achieved anything more than hearing their own false promises to themselves. These underachievers get all excited when their company announces some sort of sales incentive, boasting that they will surely win.

I worked at United States Properties with a salesman named Phil. Every month Phil enthusiastically announced that he was going to become salesman of the month, which would entitle him to some sort of monetary reward.

During the first week or so, Phil was motivated enough to work his butt off, uttering positive statements such as, "I'm really psyched this time to win," and "I know I am going to break all sales records for the month."

By the time week three rolled around, Phil was unenthusiastically mumbling platitudes like, "Why break your ass for something that you will be too tired to enjoy," and "I can't catch the breaks like Arthur and Sam." (Arthur was myself; Sam was a successful salesman at United States Properties.)

What happens to salesmen like Phil? The answer is fairly simple. These salesmen are genuinely motivated and sincere when they commit themselves to a goal; but what they lack is the persistence to sustain themselves when times get tough.

Street smart salesmen develop the necessary perseverance needed to achieve greatness by clearly defining the goals that they want to achieve, not the goals that would please others. This is a critical point. Individuals who try to reach goals that others set will not be able to sustain their motivation. Oh sure, they might appear to be enthused and motivated in the beginning, in order to please the people who are important to them, but since they have not set these goals for themselves, these objectives become less and less important as they appear to be harder and harder to reach.

Previously, we spoke about Phil, and how he wanted to become salesman of the month. He was enthused and motivated, especially after the company announced the sales incentive for that particular month. That was Phil's problem. He was only motivated after someone else set a goal for him. Phil never really had the deep-down desire of becoming a top sales producer. Inwardly he knew that he did not have the perseverance to achieve that status; if he did, he would not need someone else motivating him by setting sales goals for him. Street smart salesmen set their own personal goals that have meaning to them.

I have a cousin Richard who dropped out of medical school in order to pursue an acting career. Needless to say, my aunt and uncle wanted to kill my cousin Richard. At the time, I myself doubted Richard's wisdom of quitting (I was three years younger than Richard, struggling to pass all my college courses). A few years later, I had the opportunity to ask my cousin why he had made such a radical career move. Richard related how he had always wanted to do something creative with his life. Whenever he had gone to a movie or theatre, he had envied the actors. The only reason he attempted to become a doctor in the first place was to please his parents, and the motivation to do so ran out shortly after that first year of medical school.

Looking back I can clearly see that Richard not only made a brave decision but a street smart one. We cannot live our lives for others, for it will surely lead to a bitter road. Richard never made it as an actor, but his creativity has enabled him to become a highly successful advertising executive. Be street smart—define where you want to go.

Street smart salesmen avoid procrastination; they do not put things off. Once they define what they want to achieve, they move quickly on their ideas. These energetic salesmen are aware that procrastination will eventually lead to indifference.

Individuals who are indifferent will never have the per-severance to keep it up in order to reach their goals. When a person sets a goal, it is natural that his enthusiasm is strongest in the beginning of his efforts. This is the very reason that street smart salesmen react in a cobra-like fashion on their ideas.

The world is full of *could-of* millionaires who procrastinated their lives away. I have an uncle who swore to me that he thought of opening a fast food hamburger restaurant way before Ray Kroc ever came up with the idea of McDonald's. Every time I used to drive with my uncle and we would pass a McDonald's, he would invariably say, "Those restaurants *could of* been all mine. In fact, my hamburgers would have been ten times better then McDonald's." Whenever I questioned my uncle as to why he never pursued his idea to open a fast food restaurant, he would make one lame excuse after another and quickly change the subject to the second biggest disappointment in his life, the Dodgers' moving out of Brooklyn.

If the truth be told, my uncle never had the perseverance to allow himself the chance to achieve. He was a dreamer who became motivated for short periods of time. If someone had offered him a real opportunity, I'm sure he would have thought about it for so long that it would eventually not be there for him. Street smart salesmen are doers, not procrastinators. Become a doer; be street smart!

Street smart salesmen do not need instant gratification in order to succeed. As a result of their enormous perseverance, street smart salesmen are fighters. They know how to roll with the punches. I am most proud that, during my early days of selling, I did not give up even though I did not have a very encouraging beginning.

My very first sales appointment was with the Wilheim family. I was supposed to be at their home at seven in the evening. Not wanting to be late, I gave myself plenty of driving time in case I hit traffic. By five thirty, I was parked down the block from the Wilheim home. For the next one-and-a-half hours I practiced my sales presentation, trying to anticipate any objections that the Wilheims might come up with.

Finally, the bewitching hour arrived. Nervously, I adjusted my tie for the upteenth time, pressed my tongue against my bottom front teeth (someone on a radio talk show indicated that doing this helps to relieve tension, and in fact it does), took two deep breaths, and made my way to the Wilheims' front door.

Mr. Wilheim, a rather large man with a friendly-enough smile, greeted me. He brought me into his living room just as Walter Cronkite was about to report the evening news. As God is my witness, the following description of what happened to me in the next five minutes in the Wilheim home is 100 percent true. I had just finished introducing myself to Mrs. Wilheim when Walter Cronkite began reporting on land frauds in the Pocono Mountains (the Pocono Mountains are located in Pennsylvania). Immediately, Mr. Wilheim's smile vanished. Even though I tried valiantly to inform him that we were not part of any land scams, and not remotely situated near the Pocono Mountains, he physically, and I mean physically, threw me out of his house. There I was on the sidewalk, sitting on my butt, humiliated and depressed!

The next day I awoke panic-stricken. My hands were covered with pimply grotesque hives. Immediately I went to my doctor, fearing the worst. My doctor assured me that it was not serious. All I was suffering from was acute anxiety. My hives were so bad that I had to wear white gloves to my next appointment. I looked like a Disney character.

My next sales call was with a schoolteacher named George, who lived near Belmont race track in Queens, New York. Instantly, I was able to develop a rapport with George; being a former teacher, I am sure, was a great asset. Much to my delight, George was interested in my development and gave me a deposit on a piece of land. That following weekend, George came up to see the property. Thank God, he fell in love with it. George became my very first sale! My wife and I celebrated that evening, and amazingly enough my hives disappeared the following day, never to return again.

I have always attributed my success to the fact that my ability to persevere far exceeded my intellectual capacities. Underachievers look for instant gratification. That is the very reason they never have the discipline to persevere when things do not work out as they expected. If I had looked for instant gratification, I would have left the selling profession as soon as my butt hit the Wilheims' front walk. Be street smart—keep it up, become successful!

In summary, street smart salesmen have the discipline to persevere in order to reach their goals. They develop this perseverance by setting goals that have meaning for them, not by trying to please others. They avoid procrastination by acting quickly on their ideas. Street smart salesmen are there for the long haul, not needing instant gratification in order to sustain their motivation to succeed.

The following questions are designed to help you look within yourself to see if you are tough enough to become a street smart sales warrior. Persevere long enough to read these questions, and answer them either in your mind or on a sheet of paper.

1. Specifically, what were the last few goals that you set for yourself that you failed to reach?

2. Why did you think you failed?

3. Do you find it more difficult to continue to take action in reaching a goal once your initial enthusiasm wears off?

4. If you had a choice, would you rather be doing something else with your life?

5. What, and why?

6. Do you seem to negatively affect your performance due to procrastination?

7. If you do not succeed fairly soon in reaching an objective, do you have a tendency to quit?

8. If so, why?

It is not easy looking at yourself. It can be downright frightening. Selling may not be for you. However, if your answers are in line with what you've just read in this chapter, you've just taken a dramatic third step towards becoming a street smart salesman!

4
Like What You See

Street smart salesmen have a strong self-image, which gives them enormous confidence in their ability to achieve. They have a lust for life, believing that each day brings new opportunities; and because of this attitude, they live each day to the fullest, as if it were their last, knowing that one day they will be right! These savvy salesmen never become so negative, depressed, or disgusted with themselves that they are not able to function at their highest level. If things do not go as expected on a given day, they write it off as a learning experience. Street smart salesmen understand that yesterday is a cancelled check, while today and tomorrow are opportunities to make it happen: and street smart salesmen do indeed make it happen!

If your self-esteem is low, and you find yourself walking around feeling depressed, frustrated, and so sorry for yourself that you can't function at a high level, then it is time for you to become street smart and begin to develop a positive self-image, learning to *like what you see!*

We already have suggested that a key element for the street smart salesman to achieve great success is having a positive self-image. But what factors influence the way a person sees himself? Why do some people have high self-esteem, whereas others have extremely low self-esteem?

There are two variables, one internal and the other external, that influence the development of a person's self-esteem.

The internal factor is directly related to the way an individual perceives himself as well as the way he believes others see him. The external factors have to do with his surrounding environment, such as his job.

I will first discuss some of the internal factors. Depending on the way an individual sees himself, internal factors can either be translated into positive or negative behavior.

Underachievers do not see themselves as winners; they have a poor self-image. Their attitude is so negative about themselves that they sincerely believe failure for them is unavoidable. They have so little faith in their abilities that they lack the confidence to try to overcome their problems. Underachievers believe their problems are insurmountable.

Underachievers reinforce their negative behavior by making statements such as, "I know I'm going to fail," "I'm not going to try that; there is no way I can accomplish that." These negative self-fulfilling prophecies rob the underachiever of any confidence or motivation he might have had.

For almost six months I worked with a salesman who I will call Sal. Sal was the most self-effacing person I have ever met. It got to the point where I think Sal actually got some perverse pleasure out of putting himself down. He would even blame himself if it rained on a weekend, as if God had it in for him.

Sadly, I believe Sal had the potential to succeed, if only he had given himself a chance. Instead, Sal dwelled on the things that he did not like about himself, choosing not to see some of his positive attributes.

This is a crucial point. How many of us as a result of having a poor self-image, combined with negative thinking and lack of confidence, helplessly render ourselves into being salesmen like Sal. Underachievers do exactly that. They spend more time feeling poorly about themselves, making all sorts of excuses why they can't achieve greatness, than time putting forth a total effort in trying to overcome any of their problems.

Street smart salesmen see themselves as winners, and because of this they develop a positive self-image. They believe in their own abilities to succeed. If things do not go as expected, they don't punish themselves by putting themselves down. They never make destructive statements such as "I can't," instead choosing to say, "I will succeed."

Setbacks are viewed as a challenge to the street smart salesmen. They do not feel sorry for themselves, becoming so depressed and despondent that they can't continue to function at a high level in order to overcome any temporary obstacles that they might face. This is a key point. Street smart salesmen believe their problems are temporary roadblocks. Street smart salesmen are aware that having a strong self-image, combined with positive thinking, will go a long way in helping them to resolve any problems.

How many of you have become your own worst enemies by doubting your ability to achieve. Become street smart, wipe out ill feeling towards yourself. Talk in the positive, "I will succeed," "I know I can do that," learn to like yourself, be street smart!

Underachievers perceive that others around them see them as being inadequate, ineffective, and unqualified. This is a typical feeling for individuals who have low self-esteem. After all, if they don't think much of themselves, why should they believe anyone else would.

Unfortunately, this negative perception of how others see them adds to their depression, frustration, and despondency, making them feel nervous, uncomfortable, and embarrassed before they even have a chance to say hello to their new prospects! This defeatist attitude thoroughly destroys their confidence, making it difficult for the faker, taker, and maker to operate effectively on a day-to-day basis.

The street smart salesman is not worried about how others see him; he is more concerned with keeping a positive self-image and getting the job done. He is bright enough to know that having negative perceptions such as, "This client thinks I'm a jerk," or "Boy, am I embarrassing myself in front of this guy," is nonsense. There is nothing to be gained by this kind of thinking.

If things do not go well during a sales presentation, the street smart salesman doesn't get destroyed or embarrassed, wanting to run and hide from that client. What he wants to do is learn from his experiences and salvage whatever he can in order to try to get another opportunity to make the sale. He will not allow a poor presentation to squelch his motivation or confidence. He knows salesmen do not go to jail just because they gave a lousy sales presentation; if they did, our jails would be bursting at the seams. What is important is not to waste your time worrying about how others think about you. Rather, concentrate on how you can improve your skills; and this can only be accomplished when you have a strong, confident self-image.

As part of many Japanese sales training programs, program directors insist that their salesmen sing a song in a crowded place, such as a train station. The purpose of this exercise is to build up the salesmen's self-confidence. They get their salesmen to understand that there is nothing to be embarrassed or ashamed about, and that negative feelings about themselves are merely perceptions in their own heads that they are perfectly capable of eliminating.

If you find yourself overly concerned with how others think about you, it may be time for your singing debut. Stop worrying about how the world sees you. You will find that people will enjoy you as soon as you are confident enough to give them a chance. Be street smart—learn to like yourself; concentrate on getting the job done!

External factors can be translated into positive or negative behavior, just like the internal factors, based on the way an individual sees himself.

Street smart salesmen react positively to the external factors that influence them, whereas their underachieving counterparts react negatively to these same factors, giving themselves all sorts of excuses why they do not like their job, and why they are not able to perform.

The type of sales manager that an individual works with is an external factor that can directly influence the way a salesman performs.

Poor sales management allows mediocrity to become the standard for its sales department. This type of sales environment is comfortable to the underachiever. He doesn't feel threatened and is content enough to occasionally make a small commission over and above his weekly salary. The lack of supervision combined with the security of having a check every Friday hold the faker, taker, and maker in the job.

The street smart salesman overcomes the negative influences of working with a poor sales manager by setting up his own standards of performance. These hard-working salesmen do not allow mediocrity to keep them from achieving great success. Picking up a paycheck every Friday, void of large commissions, offers no security to the street smart salesman. The street smart salesman is not on the job to take up space; he is not on the job because the environment is nonthreatening; he is on the job for one reason only: it provides him with the opportunity and satisfaction of earning big bucks, and if it didn't, he would move on to another job.

On the other hand, an underachiever would find it impossible to survive long-term work with a strong sales manager. A capable sales manager is conscientious, and is aware of who is producing and who is not, knowing full well that it is his responsibility not to allow mediocrity to continue.

Underachievers having a low self-esteem would interpret a strong sales manager's best intentions as threatening, feeling that they are being picked on, rather than seeing it as a consequence of their inadequacies.

Street smart salesmen are only too happy to be working with capable sales managers. They see them as part of their teams, working for the same positive results.

Because the street smart salesman has a strong self-image, he does not become defensive when his sales manager offers some constructive criticism or advice. Street smart salesmen are more concerned with the bottom line than with their ego. They are smart enough to take advantage of any help that is available.

I knew a salesman who sold all sorts of tools and gadgets to hardware stores. No matter how much or how little he sold, his income basically stayed the same. There were no performance incentives.

One year, he was offered a job by one of his competitors;

through sales incentives, the job would have given him the opportunity to earn a great deal more money.

Astonishing to me, he turned the job down, for reasons that I now realize are typical of the underachiever.

Instead of seeing opportunity, he chose to concentrate on what he perceived to be the negative aspects of the job. He was uncomfortable not having a guaranteed check waiting for him each week, even though he would be in a situation that could pay him a lot more money.

He also voiced concern about the sales manager, who he felt could be very demanding. He liked being left alone; he did not want anyone on his back. Accountability was not for him.

Seven years later, he is still on the job, living from paycheck to paycheck.

A street smart salesman would have jumped at the opportunity to have a job that did not limit, for the most part, his earning potential. Street smart salesmen never think that they are going to fail—they believe in themselves, and that's all the security they need. Be street smart, be confident, become successful!

An external factor that directly influences fakers', takers', and makers' poor self-image is their feeling that they are always being looked at and put down by others.

Their perception that people are always looking and putting them down is not entirely paranoid on the part of the faker, taker, and maker. Unfortunately, underachievers do not realize that people do look at them because of their bizarre behavior or negative performances.

Underachievers would rather complain and feel sorry for themselves, preferring to blame everyone in sight for their failures except the main culprit, themselves!

A reason why fakers, takers, and makers do not like their jobs is the fact that they have become bored with the product they are selling, which totally wipes out any motivation that they might have had, making it impossible for them to achieve success. In addition to being bored selling their product, many salesmen do not believe in their product. This occurs when salesmen stop trying to learn enough about it. It is difficult to believe in something and remain excited if you have given up trying to discover all the positive things about it.

Street smart salesmen love their job, and if they didn't, they certainly would not choose to vegetate, feeling sorry for themselves; instead they would go out and find a job they would enjoy.

Street smart salesmen love the challenge of becoming the very best in their company. They find their work stimulating because it constantly creates new opportunities for them. Many times these enthusiastic salesmen will go after accounts that an underachiever would consider impossible to sell or a complete waste of time. Nevertheless, the street smart salesmen will try again and again and again to land one of these difficult accounts; and when they do, their enthusiasm and excitement for their work goes right through the roof!

It is important for the street smart salesmen to believe in the product they are selling. They are hustlers, not hucksters; they have to morally believe that their product can do the job they represent.

These savvy salesmen never stop trying to learn more about their product. It helps to keep their enthusiasm and motivation high, which gives them an edge over their competitors who have become bored, tired, and cynical.

About a year ago, on a Sunday afternoon, I was stretched out on my den couch eating pretzels, which happens to be my favorite junk snack food, watching the New York Knickerbockers attempting to beat the Boston Celtics. It was the third quarter in a close game when I heard my front doorbell ring. Quickly I ran to answer it, not wanting to miss any of the game. Much to my dismay, standing on the front porch was a young man carrying a vacuum, with all sorts of attachments coming out from every angle of his body, giving him an alien-like appearance. This had to be a mistake; no one sells vacuums on a Sunday afternoon, especially during a New York Knick, Boston Celtic basketball game. Unfortunately for me, before I could get rid of this octopus of a salesman, my wife, Sally, entered the hallway, greeted him, and quickly led this invader of my relaxation into the den to show me this vacuum.

For the next twenty minutes, this so-called vacuum salesman gave the most boring, unenthused, monotonous sales presentation that I have ever had the dissatisfaction to be in front of. It was torture. If he had continued much longer I would have had to place toothpicks under my eyelids in order to keep my eyes from closing.

I asked him right out, why he seemed to be so unenthused. This turned out to be my second biggest mistake of the day, the first being having let him in. He proceeded to whine to me, and I mean whine, how he hated schlepping this vacuum around. It was obvious that the vacuum had become his enemy. When I asked him why he continued to do this kind of work if he hated it so much, he looked at me with a bewildered look, replying that he really didn't know why, but probably because all jobs stink after awhile.

He was pathetic. There was no way that I would buy from him. Why encourage him to inflict his pain on other people.

If that vacuum salesman had been street smart, he would have been enthused and motivated to sell us. In addition, he would have treated that machine like gold, because in the hands of a street smart salesman it would have been gold.

If you are disgusted with yourself and your job, and bored with the product you are selling, quickly look for a job that will make you feel good about yourself. Only then will you achieve, but more important, you will begin to learn to like what you see in the mirror!

The negative thinking of others is the last external factor that can be detrimental to a person's self-esteem.

As previously discussed, people who are negative can dishearten and discourage individuals from trying to achieve. They tend to put labels on people, with comments such as, "Don't try that," and "There is no way you can accomplish that."

If you are having difficulties, do not ask anyone who is negative for advice. These people are unhappy with themselves and are overjoyed upon hearing about others' despair. "Misery loves company," is these demotivators' Bill of Rights, and believe me they enjoy having loads of company.

Street smart salesmen talk only to people who can have a positive effect on them. They share their concerns with individuals who they believe genuinely care about them. Eleanor Roosevelt once said, "Nobody on the face of the earth can make you feel inferior without your consent." The street smart salesman fully understands this, and as we discussed in the previous chapters, will not allow the negative thoughts of others to make him feel poorly about himself.

In summary, street smart salesmen have a positive attitude that enables them to achieve great success. These confident salesmen are more concerned with getting the job done than with worrying about what people think of them. They are problem solvers, not problem dwellers. They do not get so down on themselves that they are not able to achieve greatness. Street smart salesmen stay away from people who have a negative effect on their performance. Be street smart. If there is no one around for you to talk to who is positive, don't worry. Smile, look into the mirror, and discuss what's bothering you with someone you really like, yourself!

The following questions are designed to see if you really like who you are. Be honest; the only one you can offend is yourself, so, who cares, it's for your own benefit. Read these questions carefully and answer them either in your mind or on a sheet of paper.

1. Do you see yourself as having a positive or negative self-image?

2. How do you believe others perceive you?

3. Do you feel uncomfortable selling your product?

4. Do you believe you are living in the best of times?

5. If not, why not?

6. When you have a setback at work, do you become so depressed and despondent that you find it difficult to function at a high level in order to overcome any of those obstacles?

7. Are you more concerned with how you appear to others than you are with working towards getting the job done?

8. Do you tend to blame others for your misfortunes?

9. Are you being negatively influenced by the thoughts of others?

10. If so, how so?

Sometimes it is not easy to think about who you are. If you have a low self-esteem, a pessimistic point of view, and find yourself surrounded by people who are negative, maybe you've hit upon the reason why you haven't achieved what you want. You now have the ability to turn all these negative self-images around. As soon as you understand what changes you have to make, you will be that much closer to becoming street smart!

5
Schtick

Street smart salesmen stand out. Why? Because of their schtick. But what is schtick? Schtick is having the confidence in yourself not to be afraid to be different.

Schtick allows the street smart salesman to be as creative as he wants, since schtick has no boundaries, restrictions, barriers, or limitations. Through the use of imagination and perseverence, the street smart salesman is constantly trying to come up with new methods, which I call schtick, to set himself apart from his competition.

Since schtick can be interesting, exciting and outrageous, work is always fun for the street smart salesman, but more importantly, the street smart salesman makes it interesting and entertaining for his prospects. This is a key point: he entertains his customers, never offending them; and because they are entertained, he can get away with a lot of schtick!

If you are still using the same old selling techniques that you have used since you first started out, which by now have become boring and stale to you as well as to your prospects, it is time to develop schtick. Read this chapter with your imagination hats on, study some of the schtick that we will talk about, and get ready to have fun again in selling. Develop your own schtick, become street smart!

Street smart salesmen are the Walt Disneys of the sales profession, using their imagination to come up with clever methods to gain a competitive edge over their competition. Their clever techniques separate these savvy salesmen from the fakers, takers, and makers, who are as unique as white bread. The street smart salesmen's only competition is with themselves, constantly trying to develop better ideas to create new sales.

Underachievers have to compete with everybody, since they never use their creativity to stand out from the crowd.

When I first began selling recreational property, the company gave large monetary bonuses to any salesmen who sold a waterfront site. This interested me the most; I wanted the big bucks.

Instead of relying on company-generated leads, like everyone else, hoping by chance that I would be lucky enough to get the one person who might buy that waterfront property, I decided to take things into my own hands, and actively pursued individuals who could afford such properties.

I made the decision to zero in on the medical community, knowing that this was one group that could easily afford these waterfront properties.

I was aware that my most difficult task was to get doctors to take time out from their busy schedules to sit down long enough to listen to my presentation. I had the confidence that once I did get to see them, they would see the merits of having a place to escape to in order to relax, and what better place to relax than on the water.

After much thought I decided to fill small Ziploc bags with a mixture of sand and coffee. I typed, dead center on blank white paper, Will Rogers' famous line, "Land, once it is gone they can't manufacture it anymore," and simply signed my name.

A few days later I followed up my mailings with telephone calls, and amazingly, I was happy to discover that a large percentage of doctors came right to the phone without much effort on my part. They wanted to speak to the guy who went about sending dirt in the mail.

Initially, the other salesmen laughed at me when I went

about filling my Ziploc packets with my earthen brew. Soon the laughter stopped as I began selling waterfront after waterfront to all my doctor friends. It was not long before I became far and away the most successful salesman in the company. I soon learned that he who laughs last usually cashes the largest commission checks.

Street smart salesmen have the ability to learn from others. They make it a habit to study other imaginative and creative salesmen, which enables them to improve upon their own performances. Not all street smart salesmen have the creative talents to develop original effective schtick; what they are, is smart enough to learn from others.

The great salesmen of history have always had great schtick. Their one common characteristic has been their willingness, through trial and error, to come up with methods that clearly set them apart from their competition. This is a key point: it is very rare when an achiever will come up with schtick that will prove to be a winner the very first time. Sometimes a little fine tuning is necessary, and other times major revisions. No matter what it takes, through their imagination, motivation, and perseverence, they all have developed unique selling techniques that have made them champions in each of their fields.

These creative selling techniques may not be right for your personality; however, the purpose of studying other people's imaginative ideas is to stimulate your own creative juices.

Ben Feldman has sold nearly a billion dollars' worth of life insurance. Feldman found that his most difficult task was to get a chief executive officer (CEO) of a major corporation to sit down and listen to his presentation.

The technique Ben came up with was quite clever. Whenever he arrived at an office without having an appointment, he would hand the CEO's secretary an envelope containing five $100 bills and would ask for five minutes of the man's time. In one particular case that Feldman cites, he got in to see the executive and eventually sold him $50 million worth of life insurance. Asked about his greatest sale, Feldman replied, "I don't know. I haven't made it yet." This is a street smart attitude at its very best.

Joe Girard sold an average of eighteen cars a week—this does not include fleet sales—for fourteen years, making him the most successful car salesman ever.

Joe was always prospecting and selling, no matter where he was. Whenever Joe attended a sporting event, he would bring thousands and thousands of business cards, which he would toss in the air whenever the crowd stood to applaud a special play. Invariably, someone at the game either needed or knew someone who wanted to buy a new car. Joe took advantage of every possible opportunity.

Lastly, I worked with a salesman named Lenny Bieler. Lenny's schtick was to give his prospects one red rose. Often, their first response was anything but positive, questioning why Lenny would bother them with this sort of nonsense. Calmly, Lenny would reply, "I have been trying to see you for the longest of times, and because you are so busy I needed my friend the rose to help me out, and I guess it worked. Now that I am here, believe me I am glad I did bring my friend along."

Lenny would then go into his presentation, and the majority of times his prospects appreciated this clever approach, giving Lenny the opportunity needed to achieve success.

The next two salesmen are not as flamboyant as Feldman, Girard, or Bieler; nevertheless, they developed schtick that was clever, subtle, and as effective as any I have ever seen. One salesman sold college text books, the other consulting services.

The key to the success of a college book salesman is to get his text books read by the department's course coordinators, who make the decisions on which books will be used the following year. College professors do not want to sit through sales presentations, preferring to have the various book salesmen leave their texts behind so that they can peruse them at their own convenience.

The problem our book salesman had to overcome, since there were so many other salesmen also leaving their books, making it virtually impossible for a professor to evaluate each and every book, was to get that department head to read his book.

The schtick used by our clever book salesman, who in this

case is a street smart woman, was rather simple. She would leave her text books, like everyone else, on the professor's desk, with one exception. She would tie a bright green ribbon around each of her books. Guess whose books were always read? This schtick made our book saleswoman tops in her field.

The key to selling consulting services is to get to see the chief executive officer, who for the most part is extremely busy and hassled. He has no interest in hearing how other people are going to show him how to run his company more efficiently. To get to see these executives is next to impossible, except for our consulting salesman.

The schtick used by our consulting salesman was to let his dress do the talking for him. He would walk into the outer office of the CEO that he wanted to see, never having an appointment, and announce to the executive secretary that he would like to see whomever ran the company. His schtick was the fact that he would always be wearing a brown derby hat, all the while carrying a black lacquered walking cane with highly polished gold tips. Instead of brushing him off, these executive secretaries would run into their bosses' offices to see if they would like to talk to a rather odd-looking gentleman.

You might be self-conscious dressing in this manner, but I can tell you this, that brown derby and walking stick got to see an awful lot of top CEO's, helping our consulting salesman earn large commission checks.

These three salesmen are excellent examples of how using creativity helps salespeople stand out from the crowd.

Ideas for schtick can come from sources other than watching other salesmen. You can develop schtick by reading books or magazines, or even by watching a movie.

In the movie *Wall Street*, Charlie Sheen portrays an up-and-coming Wall Street broker.

Sheen has been desperately trying to set up an appointment with a powerful financier, played by Michael Douglas. Realizing that his efforts would be fruitless if he continued to try and see Douglas through conventional means, he decided to use some schtick to make it happen.

After doing some research, he was able to find out when

Douglas' birthday was. He waited for his opportunity, and the day of Douglas' birthday Sheen showed up at Douglas' office carrying a box of very expensive cigars, informing Douglas' secretary that he would like to hand-deliver his present.

The secretary took the box of cigars and walked into the financier's office, quickly returning with the news Sheen wanted to hear. Douglas had said that Sheen just bought himself five minutes.

Sheen's schtick worked; five minutes was all the time he needed!

I knew a salesman who used the library as a source in order to develop an effective schtick. He had zero personality, and he knew it as well, which made him very street smart. This fellow took out a book of jokes, which he in turn memorized. His schtick soon became one of a comedian. His customers looked forward to seeing him, knowing that he would have one or two jokes to tell them.

The key point is that schtick can come from anywhere; use it, set yourself apart from your competition.

Street smart salesmen are aware that no one ever became a leader in his field by doing what was expected. Rousseau once said, "The world of reality has its limits; the world of imagination is boundless." Use your imagination, become street smart!

The following questions are designed to help you start to use your creativity. Don't be afraid to use your imagination. This doesn't mean that you have to become, as Steve Martin would say, "a wild and crazy guy." Tying a green ribbon around a text book was not outrageous, but nevertheless, proved to be very effective for our saleswoman. The schtick that you employ should be in keeping with your own personality. The important thing is for you to be creative and not continue to be an ordinary Joe. Become imaginative—it will earn you those large commission checks.

Read these questions carefully and answer them either in your mind or on a sheet of paper.

1. Do you have any schtick?

2. Do you know anyone else who has schtick?

3. If so, what?

4. Would you find it uncomfortable as well as embarrassing to use a sales method that was out of the ordinary?

5. If so, why so?

6. Can you think of anything to do that can set you apart from your competition?

7. If not, why not?

8. Where would you look to find some inspiration for developing your own creative selling techniques?

Now that you have finished reading this chapter, you know how important it is to develop a selling technique that will set you apart from your competition. If you find that creative selling would not be too uncomfortable or embarrassing, but rather a lot of fun, you have taken a major step towards becoming street smart.

Scott Gutterson

Scott Gutterson is a highly successful street smart tax attorney. Photographs of many of his sports celebrity clients cover the walls of his New York office. It is a virtual who's who of the sporting world.

Upon graduating from law school, Scott began working for an accounting firm in Manhattan. Dressed in his Brooks Brothers suit and wing tip shoes, Scott looked like thousands of other new graduates beginning their career in the conservative world of finance. But Scott was different; he was street smart. From the very beginning, his goal was to listen, learn, and gain the experience that he would need before he could start his own practice. He knew there were many opportunities out in the business world for people with his motivation and determination; and, because he was street smart, he was not afraid to go after them. Scott indicated that he was not the type of person who would be happy working for a whole year hoping to get a cost-of-living raise. That is not him; he wanted more.

What made Scott so street smart was the fact that he understood that even though he was a tax attorney, a professional, he still was foremost in the selling business. He knew that he could be the smartest tax attorney in all the world, but unless he had the ability to sell himself and obtain clients, not enough people would be aware of his abilities, and he would starve. And, like all street smart salesmen, Scott was not going to starve.

Scott was aware that if he was going to build a thriving practice, he would have to develop an aggressive street smart prospecting program. He joined organizations that would give him the kind of exposure necessary to attract potential clients. Scott did not just take up space in these organizations. He volunteered to head and work on committees that were needed. He was not concerned about the extra work that it might entail. All he was interested in was to get his name known to people who might be able to utilize his services. Wherever he went, he left his business card. He networked his friends, relatives, school chums, and clients. As a result of all his efforts, he was able to build up his practice fairly quickly.

Scott, being street smart, wanted to develop a style that would set him apart from other tax attorneys. Shrewdly, he knew this would also help him gain additional clients. The tax attorneys that he knew and worked with were very conservative in their actions and dress. Doing business with them was not much fun. Scott also was aware that individuals did not normally look forward to visiting their accountant. Scott stated that frequently clients would come to his office nervous and scared to death that the Internal Revenue Service was about to take everything away from them. Scott was aware that a key to building his practice was to get his prospects to relax. Once they were relaxed, he could build rapport and trust.

Upon entering his office, you no longer will be greeted by an individual wearing Brooks Brothers suits and wing tipped shoes. Instead, you will be greeted by an individual wearing a San Francisco or New York Yankees baseball cap, a sweater, and Reebok sneakers, who at any moment might stop what he is doing and begin singing to a tune that is being played on the radio.

Scott has not gone crazy. Scott is one street smart salesman. His schtick has enabled him to accomplish just what he wanted to do—set himself apart from other tax accountants and make a name for himself. By not acting like a typical tax accountant, he is able to relax his clients. They have fun coming to his office; they enjoy doing business with him. More important to Scott, they tell other people about their crazy accountant who takes the pain out of dealing with their financial concerns. Often, Scott's first discussion with a client has little to do with his financial concerns. Being street smart, he gets clients talking about things they enjoy. This helps to build rapport between him and his clients. He tells them, "There is no problem that can't be solved. If they could put a man on the moon, we certainly can solve any problem. So stop being a nervous wreck." And, most important, Scott believes that to be true.

Scott, like all street smart salesmen, keeps complete files on all of his clients, making specific notations about all of their interests. If, at any time during the year, he is able to do something special for a client, Scott will do it. For example, one of his clients happens to be a tremendous Chicago Cubs base-ball fan. Coincidentally, Scott is friends with Mr. Cub, Ernie Banks, and once arranged for the three of them to have dinner together. His client was thrilled to death, sitting at the same table with his boyhood idol. Another time he took a client who enjoyed wine to a wine-tasting party. Scott, being street smart, makes it a practice to recognize his clients' interests or accomplish-ments; and, as a result, they are constantly referring other clients to him. Just imagine how many people that Cubs fan told about how his accountant arranged for him to have dinner with Ernie Banks.

By being a creative street smart salesman, Scott has been able to develop a highly lucrative and successful tax practice. A practice that is fun for him as well as his clients.

6
Money-Making Rejection

Street smart salesmen have an enormous amount of resiliency, enabling them to deal with rejection on a daily basis. Day after day, their customers try to beat them down in some fashion, but street smart salesmen persist long enough to walk away with large commissions.

Fakers, takers, and makers can't deal with rejection very well; it sends them right to their psychiatrists' couches. Underachievers need to have the approval of others. They base their self-worth upon it.

Street smart salesmen know that basing your self-worth upon others' approval is nonsense. Their goal is self-approval, trusting their own actions. These self-confident salesmen are aware that having an attitude like the underachiever's will only be asking for a life of misery and frustration, making it impossible for them to handle rejection, because in a sense they will be rejecting themselves.

Street smart salesmen know that if you are going to succeed and stay in sales for the long term, it is essential for you to deal positively with rejection. The greater your ability to handle failure and rejection on a daily basis, the more likely you can achieve greatness.

If you are finding it difficult to motivate yourself to achieve after hearing the word "no" from one of your prospects, it is time to learn how to deal positively with rejection. Become street smart, turn a "no" into a *money-making rejection*.

Street smart salesmen never take rejection personally. When a prospect says "no" to a street smart salesman, he interprets it as a challenge to try to overcome his prospect's objections in order to make the sale.

When a client says "no," the street smart salesman understands this to mean, "maybe," "perhaps," or "Tell me more, I'm not convinced yet." Street smart salesmen never, never, never consider "no" to mean, "I definitely will never do business with you." This is the very reason why they have no difficulty going back time and again to their prospects.

When will a street smart salesman finally give up? When his customers learn to enunciate the word "Yes!"

Fakers, takers, and makers are totally destroyed when they get rejected. These underachievers hear the word "no" so loudly it reverberates in their heads, as if they were in an echo chamber. Underachievers take rejection so personally that at times, as amazing as this might sound, they are hesitant to even ask for the order because of their fear of hearing the word "no." When they hear the word "no," they interpret it as, "This guy hates me," "He thinks I'm stupid," or "He'll never want to see me again."

My father has a cousin who used to sell piece goods. According to my dad, his cousin's greatest asset as a salesman was the fact that he never took no for an answer. He would go back again and again and again to the very same accounts that continually rejected him, until finally, as he put it, he wore them down and was able to get an order.

Like my dad's cousin, the street smart salesman believes just because someone says "no" one time, doesn't mean he will say "no" the next time.

Astonishingly, most children, before entering school, start off as street smart salesmen. They never hear the word "no." Kids are not looking for the approval of others; "no" doesn't phase them in the least. They come back again and again, nagging a parent to death in order to get their way. And like the street smart salesmen who are able to persevere, on many occasions kids are able to wear down their parents in order to close their sales!

What turns a child who handles rejection as easily as if he were shooting fish in a barrel, into a nervous wreck whenever he suspects the least bit of rejection? It begins when we enter grade school, leaving behind the security of mommy and daddy who love us to death and think everything we do is cute.

We start playing with other children. Quickly we learn that the kids who may be a little different, not quite adjusted to leaving mommy, are the ones who get picked on, sending them home crying each day. We don't want this grief; we want to be liked; and we'll do most anything to be accepted.

Underachievers, like the gradeschool child, will do most anything to gain the approval of others. Fakers, takers, and makers have never been able to overcome their fear of rejection.

The street smart salesman also wants to be accepted by his peers, but as he gets older he puts limits on it. He will not allow peer pressure to negatively influence his performance. Even as a young adult, the street smart salesman knew that the need to be liked was not as important as liking himself!

Street smart salesmen are not afraid to find out why they did not get the order. They have learned that a prospect for the most part will be only too happy to tell them why he doesn't want to do business with them. Street smart salesmen realize that this information can be invaluable and at times can be used at that very moment to overcome a client's objection in order to make a sale.

Even if the street smart salesmen cannot use the information at that very moment to make a sale, they certainly can use it in the future. The key is finding out what the problem is and working on a solution, be it delivery, quality, price, or themselves as salesmen.

Street smart salesmen are not so sensitive to rejection that they will allow criticism to destroy their chances of making money with that particular client in the future.

Underachievers, upon hearing the word "no" quickly pack up their wares and leave their prospect, too afraid to find out exactly why they did not get the order. Because of their fear of rejection, they eliminate enormous future opportunities for themselves.

A clever technique that the street smart salesman employs in order to avoid the frustrations that are associated with rejection, is to put a money value on every presentation that he makes. Therefore, the street smart salesman believes he earns money even if he does not close a sale. This well-adjusted salesman knows that no one is able to sell everybody the first time, and expects to get a certain amount of "no's" before he gets a "yes."

Let's suppose a salesman earns a thousand dollars in commission every time he completes a sale. In this particular example, this salesman is aware that he sells one out of four prospects that he sees. If that be the case, how much money did he earn if he saw three people who did not buy from him?

Underachievers will always say that the salesman did not earn anything. The street smart salesman will always say that the salesman earned $750; that is why he never feels rejected on a sales call. He knows that every no that he gets on a sales call gets him that much closer to a yes. In the example above, the street smart salesman understands that over the year his closing percentage would be one out of four. Before he makes a sale, he will get three "no's." That is why he is convinced that every sales presentation that he makes is earning him money. It is part of the job. It's part of the process that he has to go through before he reaches his goal, so why not get paid for it. He chooses to call a presentation that is not successful a money-making rejection.

Street smart salesmen know that rejection is part of life, and the greater their ability to handle rejection, the more likely they will be able to achieve success.

Be like the street smart salesmen—never reject yourself in order to gain the approval of others. Do not take it personally when you hear the word "no" from one of your prospects. Remember, to the street smart salesmen, a "no" today is a "yes" tomorrow!

The following questions are designed to give you some insight as to the effect that rejection may have on your performance. Read these questions carefully and answer them either in your mind or on a sheet of paper.

1. Do you find that it is important for you to be accepted by others, even though it may require you to reject some of your own ideas?

2. If so, why so?

3. Do you get depressed when a client says no to you?

4. How many times would you go back to a client before giving up?

5. Would you feel uncomfortable asking a client why he would not do business with you?

6. If so, why so?

Now that you have finished reading this chapter, you know that the word "no" in sales has many different connotations to the street smart salesman, all of which he never takes personally.

If you still have found that handling the day-to-day rejection, which is part and parcel of sales, is too depressing and frustrating, sales may not be for you. However, if you have found that your answers are in line with the thinking in this chapter, then you have taken a sixth giant step towards becoming a street smart salesman!

PART II
Skills of
the Street Smart Salesman

Before you turn your attention away from Part I and to Part II, "Skills of the Street Smart Salesman," I want you to understand that each and every one of the elements that I wrote about in part one is important if you are going to achieve greatness. However, only when these elements become integrated into your method of selling will they prove to be invaluable to you.

If you can remember learning to drive a car, you took a little while getting adjusted to the various mirrors, brakes, etc. The same holds true for these elements. You might have to practice each element separately until you find that you are comfortable with each one. Once that happens, they will soon all become integrated as if they were a fine-tuned machine.

The second half of *The Street Smart Salesman* will provide you with specific tactics that you can use in order to be able to implement the various elements that you have just read about.

Because each one of us is different, coming from different environments as well as selling different products or services, I can't expect every bit of information that I have written about to apply to each and every one of you.

The tactics have been set up to give you many different ideas that have been tried and true. If one doesn't work for you, try the next one. If the next one doesn't work, move on to another, until you find the tactics that fit into your personality, product, or service.

7
Prospecting

To a salesman, prospecting, in a manner of speaking, is like looking for gold. Instead of digging into the earth, prospecting is searching for individuals who have the need and the ability to purchase a product or service. Like the prospector who stakes his claim, a salesman with a rich supply of qualified leads has the potential to earn his fortune.

A salesman without leads or people to talk to is like a fish without water. Neither can survive very long. Yet, a common problem among most salesmen is a lack of sufficient leads. Underachievers have a great deal of difficulty deciding where to find qualified prospects. Well, where do all those wonderful leads come from? Good question, no, an excellent question. Let me tell you. Those wonderful leads stem from four things:

First, though this is rare in today's market, your product may be so good that it sells itself. More often, this occurs when your company happens to put out that one product that becomes a national fad, such as a certain jean, or an item like a Hula Hoop or Rubik's cube.

Second, the company you are working for may have a program that will produce leads, either through media, direct mail, or print advertising. An organization like the Encyclopedia Britannica is a good example of a company that spends a lot of dollars to generate a good supply of qualified leads for its salesmen.

The third way leads can come is from your own circle of friends, family, and acquaintances. Some industries base their sales projections on the principle that new salesmen will sell to many people that they know. These companies are constantly hiring because of this fact. They also know that many salesmen will fail once they are through selling to people within their circle.

The fourth way that you can get leads is on your own. This separates the achievers from the underachievers. Street smart salesmen learn never to count on the first three sources of acquiring leads. They know that they themselves are the greatest source for their own leads.

Part of the problem that faces underachievers is that they do not know how to prospect. They had counted so heavily in the past on company support for their leads that they have failed miserably in developing their own program. When their company, for whatever reason, is in a short supply of leads, their sales production goes down dramatically. Street smart salesmen will not allow this to happen. They do not depend solely on company-generated leads. When other salesmen are sitting around the office hoping to see people, street smart salesmen are busy telling their story to qualified buyers. These adroit salesmen are only able to do this because they use sources other than their company to generate leads. If you are currently dependent on others to produce leads for you, read this chapter carefully. Discover all the outside sources that are available so that you can develop your own lead-generation program. Learn the street smart tactics for prospecting. No longer will you wake up on a particular day and not know where to go and with whom to talk. Be street smart, pan for the gold; it will be well worth your effort.

❑ REFERRALS

Street smart salesmen are keenly aware that a prospect that is referred by an existing client who is happy with your product or service is a heck of a lot easier to sell than a new lead who knows very little about you and your company. Understanding this, street smart salesmen use their existing client base to obtain many qualified leads.

There is a skill in asking customers for referrals. Merely requesting, "Do you know anyone who can use my service?" will not do the trick. What you are doing is asking that client to make a judgment as to whether he knows someone who is ready to buy your product or service. In most instances, it is not possible for him to know. That is the reason why many clients with the best intentions will answer "no."

Aware of this, street smart salesmen ask clients if they belong to any business organizations, clubs, charities, etc. If their client is in an office building that has other tenants, they ask whom the client knows in the building. The theory behind this is simply that most of us surround ourselves with individuals who have similar interests, earning power, preferences, and needs. By asking for referrals in this manner, your client doesn't have to think of anything more than supplying you with names. And that's the name of the game, getting people to talk to. Remember, it is your job to do the qualifying and selling, not your client's job.

Street smart salesmen know that the best time to ask for referrals is right after the sale. At that point, your customer's enthusiasm and satisfaction are at their highest.

When I feel that I have developed a strong rapport with a client, I often ask him if he would mind telephoning his friends and telling them about me. If a client responds that he is not comfortable doing this, I then ask him if it is okay if I use his name when telephoning. In some cases, he might indicate that he also would not be comfortable with this, in which case I wouldn't use his name. In most cases, however, you will find that your customers will only be too happy to help you.

Because referrals are so essential to your success, you should always stay in touch with your old clients. Send them birthday and holiday cards. Call them up to see how they are doing. If there is a problem, take care of it promptly. Stop in to see them. Let them know that you haven't forgotten them simply because they already bought.

Be street smart, never forget that every one of your customers who own or use your product or service just might know someone who can utilize it as well.

❏ BIRD-DOGS

A bird-dog is a dog that finds birds for hunters before and after they are shot from the sky. A sales bird-dog is an individual who "beats the bushes," so to speak, to find qualified prospects for a salesman who will pay him a commission if he makes the sale. Bird-dogs can be extremely effective. They will speak to everybody, just so they will have an opportunity to make some extra money.

Bird-dogs can be relatives, friends, the postman, past clients, etc. These individuals can be an excellent source of leads. Enlist as many bird-dogs as you can. It's the street smart thing to do.

❏ NETWORKING

Networking is when you become your own best bird-dog. Wherever you go, you simply get the word out as to what you do for a living. This includes your barber, attorney, banker, etc. Don't be embarrassed; you never know where your next referral will come from.

Street smart salesmen maximize their networking abilities by joining organizations that put them in contact with potential clients. These expert salesmen increase their exposure in these organizations by becoming active members. This may include doing volunteer work or heading specific committees. These organizations can be charities, business associations, country clubs, sporting activities, etc.

Be street smart—wherever you go, make sure your business cards are readily available. Get the word out!

❏ TRADING LEADS

An excellent method of prospecting is to set up a system whereby you trade leads with other salesmen who sell to the same market as you do. For example, home improvement and appliance salesmen can have an effective trading program. People who do work on their homes are often in the market for new appliances and vice versa.

Analyze who your customers are. Then list all the other products or services they might utilize. After your list is compiled, you can then go about trying to set up a trading network between you and the other salesmen.

❏ LISTS

Street smart salesmen utilize all kinds of lists of businesses and people in their day-to-day prospecting. These lists are readily available through your local libraries as well as professional list brokers.

Locate a library that has a strong business section. You will find directories that cover just about everything. It is essential for you to learn how to use these sources. Don't be afraid to ask a librarian for assistance. The following examples of directories will give you a good indication of how effective these books can be:

- *Reverse Directories.* These are cross–reference directories. They allow you to prospect in a specific geographical area. These publications list telephone numbers in order of street, house number, town, country, or phone number itself. The *Cole Directory* is an excellent cross-reference directory.

- *SIC Classifications.* Prospecting by Standard Industrial Classification (SIC) code number can be very effective. Each type of business has a separate SIC number. Related businesses have similar numbers so that you can scan through a directory and choose only the numbers that apply to the product or service that you are selling. This not only will provide you with an excellent list, but in addition, will give you insight into other related industries that you might be able to solicit, but of which you were not yet aware.

- *Corporate Directories.* These types of directories give excellent analyses of corporations. They can include company size, type of business, sales volume, principals, and titles. Dun and Bradstreet's *Million Dollar Directory* and Moody's *Standard and Poor*'s are excellent sources. *Million Dollar Directory* lists 160,000 businesses with a net worth of more than $500,000. Ward's *Business Directory* lists private and public companies throughout the United States with annual sales of $5,000,000 or more.

- *Specialized Directories.* There are directories that list individuals according to profession. The Martindale *Hubbell Law Directory* lists attorneys according to state. The American Medical Association publishes the *American Medical Directory,* which lists physicians in the United States.

It would be impossible to list all the sources that you can go to. What I have tried to accomplish is to get you to understand that there are enormous amounts of material out there that can be invaluable to you in your prospecting. The first reference book that you should use is *Directories In Print.* It is a guide to approximately 10,000 business and industrial directories. It should point you in the right direction.

If for some reason you cannot locate the list that you need, there are literally hundreds of list brokers who will secure for you what you need. Dun and Bradstreet is one such example.

❑ PROSPECTING BY TELEPHONE

If ever there were a national salesmen's award show, it would definitely have to be named after Alexander Graham Bell. The telephone, invented by Bell, is by far the greatest sales tool.

Because of the telephone, salesmen can prospect not only in their own town, but throughout the world.

Amazingly, many salesmen do not take advantage of the telephone. In fact, a great many salesmen will not take a job, no matter how great the potential, if they have to generate their own leads. Not street smart salesmen. They know that the telephone is the most effective tool they have in reaching people. Instead of sitting around hoping to get company-generated leads, these artful salesmen are constantly on the telephone trying to make appointments to tell their story.

If the telephone does not play a large part in your sales program, read this section carefully. It will give you street smart tactics on how to maximize your telephone prospecting techniques.

When using the telephone, you must be conscious of how you sound and the words that you use. A prospect whom you are calling for the first time to set up an appointment can only judge you by your voice. Your prospect cannot see you, your product, brochures, or any other aids that will help you on your face-to-face sales call. So, if he hears a salesman who has a boring, monotonous voice, with poor diction, he most likely will choose not to see you.

Street smart salesmen always sound enthused when speaking to a prospect. Their enunciation is clear so they can be easily understood. These skillful salesmen choose their words carefully, trying to paint clear mental pictures of opportunity to their prospects. They get appointments because they create interest on the telephone.

Street smart salesmen who have the ability to talk in certain dialects use them effectively on the telephone. It helps to gain the attention of their prospects. This is how it works. When a prospect comes to the telephone, he expects to hear a familiar speech pattern that is germane to his area. A Boston, New York, Southern, or Midwestern accent is not an accent in his part of the country. For example, a prospect from New York, upon hearing a Southern accent, will give you a few extra seconds to make your impression simply because he is surprised and somewhat intrigued by the sound of your voice.

Those few extra seconds can make the difference in getting the appointment or not. Many street smart salesmen will employ an English accent on the telephone. This not only sets them apart from the typical salesmen, but to Americans, a British accent conveys a feeling of intelligence. Prospects like to speak to intelligent people.

If you decide to use the tactic of dialect, make sure that you use a different name when calling. You are the associate calling to set up appointments for so-and-so. You don't want to show up at an appointment with the wrong voice.

Never ad-lib your telephone presentations, using different approaches each time you speak to a prospect. Your presentation on the telephone should be well-scripted. It should include a question or two that will engage your prospect in a short conversation. The word *convert* comes from *conver*sation. With conversation you have a better chance of converting your phone call into an appointment. In addition, you should be prepared to answer any objections that might come up. Role play with friends, relatives, or colleagues until you feel and sound natural and comfortable.

Remember, when you call for an appointment, you are not trying to sell your product or service on the telephone. Your only purpose is to get an appointment, nothing more. If a prospect asks you for information that could lead you to tell more, then you should use this response, "That's why I am calling, to set up an appointment to cover these types of things."

Prospects will try to find out how much your product or service will cost before seeing you. This can severely hurt your chances of getting an appointment, since they will be making their judgment strictly on price. Here is a street smart answer to such a question:

Salesman: Before I answer your question on price, let me ask you a question. George, how much will you give me for my 1985 Pontiac?

Prospect: How can I say; I have to see it.

Salesman: Exactly, George, and it is the same with my product. You have to see and hear what it can do for you.

Prospects will often ask you to send them brochures. For the most part, that is a kiss-off and a waste of your time. The street smart answer to this request is, "George, our brochure is 5'11" and weighs 185 pounds; what day is better, Monday or Wednesday, to drop it off?" If you do not come off sounding like a smart aleck, it can be very effective. Often your prospect will laugh and give you your appointment.

In order to have an effective prospecting program using the telephone, you must set up specific times to call each day. If you are not disciplined in your telephoning, it will become an ad hoc tool and eventually will not be used often enough to have any sustained value.

Be street smart; take advantage of Alexander Graham Bell's invention, and dial for dollars!

❑ CANVASSING

Canvassing can be an effective way of prospecting if used wisely. I am not an advocate of getting up in the morning and knocking cold on doors. It's not a productive use of time. Utilizing the telephone, I believe, is a much wiser and more effective way of using your energies. But if you find yourself in an office building after finishing a sales call, stop in to the other offices and introduce yourself. At times, you may even get an opportunity to give a sales talk. If not, at least find out the name of the person whom you would like to see. Leave your card or brochure, indicating to his/her secretary that you will be following up with a telephone call to set up an appointment.

The important point is that you obtain the name of the individual to whom you need to speak, as well as his secretary's name. When calling back, it sometimes helps you to get through to the person you want to speak to by having the secretary's name. "Hello, Betty, is Mr. Brown in?" This gives the impression that you know her as well as Mr. Brown. In some instances, even though she does not recognize your voice, she will put you through to Mr. Brown, not wanting to admit that she has forgotten who you are. This does not happen often, but whatever edge we can gain, we as street smart salesmen will take.

❏ DIRECT MAIL

Direct mail—sending brochures, letters, or what-have-you—is another way of prospecting for customers. The down side to this program is that people in business, just like homeowners, are besieged with all sorts of direct mail pieces. If your letter or mailing piece is not clever or different, you will not get the results. It will get thrown out with tons of other junk mail pieces.

Street smart salesmen will handwrite the address on the envelope in order to personalize their material. Prospects are not so inclined to throw out a piece of mail without opening it if it is handwritten.

Street smart salesmen will frequently write their introductory letter on stationery without a letterhead. This tactic is used to insure that the prospect will read at least the first line or two. Think about it: how often do you throw away a mailing piece right after you glance at the letterhead? If you use a mailing piece, make sure that the first sentence or two will catch your prospect's interest.

Street smart salesmen will often telephone the people to whom they have sent a direct mail piece. This approach definitely increases their prospecting results. After all, they are taking an aggressive approach, and are not just waiting for a potential customer to contact them.

Direct mail should be used to supplement your prospecting methods. Do not rely solely on it to gain new leads.

❏ SPECIAL PROMOTIONS

Trade and consumer shows are an excellent way of gaining leads. Trade shows are usually sponsored by the industry that your company belongs to. People who attend these shows are excited to see the advances and new products that have been developed during the year. To attract the attention of the people, companies spend a great deal of money on their display booths.

Many salesmen avoid working these shows because they usually require travel and long hours. If you are given the opportunity to work an industry show, do it. It is an excellent place to make contacts with potential customers. It is a lot more effective, when calling up a person for an appointment, to have already met him face to face.

Consumer shows are slightly different. They are not industry based and are open for the general public. They can be antique shows, auto shows, home-improvement shows, flea markets, etc. Many different kinds of products and services are usually offered. What is important about these shows is that they usually draw a lot of people. And where there are people, there are potential customers. Search out these shows. Pick the ones that will benefit you the most.

When I first began selling recreational property, I built my own booth that consisted of a few pictures of vacant property. On top of a counter, I had a huge pile of dirt with a sign over it saying, "For Sale." I set this display up in my local flea market. My colleagues said I was wasting my time. I knew better; and after I began making sales, my fellow salesmen did the same.

Be street smart, get out to the people. That's where the action is.

❏ NEWSPAPERS

Street smart salesmen use newspapers to prospect. The newspaper can give you valuable information about people and companies.

Newspapers report on who has been promoted. They reveal if a celebrity is moving into the area. This information can be invaluable to a salesman selling insurance, home-improvements, real estate, etc.

Newspapers run ads for companies looking to hire. Companies that hire are usually expanding, which may prove helpful to a salesman who does recruiting, office sales, real estate, etc.

Read the paper with a prospecting eye; it is the street smart thing to do.

❏ TURNOVER

At some time or another, all companies experience turnover in their sales department. When this occurs, what do you think the salesmen leave behind? Right, their customer lists. Don't let these lists sit idle. Ask your sales manager if you can go through the files and see if you can develop business.

If a prospect informs you that he stopped doing business because he was not happy with the way he was handled, tell him that is the exact reason you were assigned to his company. To provide him with the best service possible.

❏ OLD CUSTOMERS

Street smart salesmen prospect by calling old clients. Most products have a life cycle, and it is your job to figure out when your prospect will be in the market again. If you sell cars, ask your customer at the time of purchase how often he purchases a new automobile. Make note of this information on your customer card.

Because products or services having long life cycles are infrequent or one-time sales, you can be remembered as your client's sole supplier by keeping in touch with him and asking how these products are holding up. When others ask him if he knows where to get a particular item, it will be you that he recommends. If there have been technical advances made on your product, inform your customers about them. It is human nature to want the newest and the best.

Be street smart, don't always look for new faces. Some of the old ones might be very rewarding.

In summary, the end product of all this action that I have described is to get an individual to buy whatever it is you are selling. Street smart salesmen know that the more people they see, the better are their chances of earning those large commission checks. Don't cut down your chances by depending on your company to supply you with prospects. Go out and make it happen for yourself by employing these street smart prospecting tactics.

The following questions are designed to get you to prospect like a street smart salesman. Read these questions carefully and answer them either in your mind or on a sheet of paper.

1. What percentage of your day is set aside for prospecting?

2. What methods do you use to prospect for customers?

3. Currently, what type of prospecting produces the most leads for you?

4. Do you depend solely on company-generated leads? If so, why so?

5. What type of prospecting do you think could be more effective with the type of product or service you represent?

6. What is the life cycle of your product?

7. Are you successful in obtaining referrals from clients? If not, why not?

8. Do you have a well-scripted telephone presentation? If not, why not?

Now that you have completed this chapter, you should realize that you do not have to depend solely on company-generated leads to see potential prospects. In fact, the less you depend on your company, the more you will earn. Street smart salesmen are successful because they are not satisfied with what their company can do for them with respect to leads. They are not content to sit back and hope that their company can supply them with sufficient leads to make a living. Street smart salesmen are looking to make much more than a living.

If after reading all these prospecting techniques, you still find that you would not be comfortable prospecting, then selling may not be for you. However, if you are excited and enthused about all the fantastic opportunities out there for you, then you have taken a major step towards becoming a street smart salesman!

Eugene Dreyfuss and Douglas Szalai

Gene Dreyfuss and Doug Szalai started Delson Business Systems, Inc., in 1972. Today, Delson is one of the largest dealers of photocopiers and facsimile machines in the tri-state area of New York. Its annual revenues are $32 million. Gene and Doug are highly successful street smart businessmen, yet when they first met while working as salesmen for the same company, they had little more than a dream.

The company that they first worked for had poor sales supervision. This surprised Gene and Doug, because as part of their early training they had been sent to seminars that taught the importance of time and territorial management. Nevertheless, salesmen were given little direction, and were allowed to operate pretty much on their own. Performance standards and goals were never discussed. As a result, many of the salesmen lacked motivation to achieve. Mediocrity became the standard. Eugene and Doug did not want any part of this. They put the lessons that they had learned at their time and territorial management seminars to practical use. Even though they were the two top salesmen in the company, they were still able to plan their own business venture.

The venture that Gene and Doug decided to go into was the business machine supply business, carrying products such as toners, paper, and ribbons. But, because they were street smart and listened to what their customers had to say, they quickly discovered that there was a greater need for a reliable business machine company than one selling photocopy paper. Their clients told them that the companies they were presently doing business with did not keep their promises; there was a high turnover of sales staff; therefore, relationships were not being built. By asking the right questions, Gene and Doug learned that if they wanted a successful business machine company, it was critical for them to have back-up personnel to service the equipment. Knowing this, and being street smart, they hired two service people even before they had their first client. They were determined to provide the best service in the industry. Today, 80 percent of their employees are in service-oriented positions, guaranteeing that this philosophy of service and support for their customers will be met.

It was not easy starting this new business machine venture. Like many companies, in their early stages, they did not have a lot of capital. What they had was street smart perseverance and a station wagon. Their perseverance allowed them to work long hours prospecting for new business. They went from office building to office building searching for new prospects. They networked their friends and past clients to get leads. They read the business sections of the newspapers to see if companies were relocating into their market. Prospecting for business was a daily routine of theirs. The station wagon allowed them to take their business machines with them on their sales calls. A customer could actually see what that machine was capable of doing. If, after the demonstration, their prospect was still undecided, they would leave the machine behind so that the prospect could utilize the benefits for a few days. They gambled that once a person gets used to the better things in life, it is difficult to give them up. And their street smart gamble paid off. Companies kept their machines, and liked doing business with them. They were growing rapidly.

Even though their product knowledge was limited in the beginning of their business, Gene and Doug were still able to put together the best product line available. This was accomplished because they are street smart salesmen, and were able to ask their prospects the right questions. Their prospects actually told them what business machines were the best in the field. This education was critical to their early success. It would have been devastating if they had invested in equipment that would not deliver the goods.

Being street smart, Gene and Doug's goals were always well-defined. This insured that they would not be operating on vague hopes and wishes. These goals continue to keep them focused and give them the incentive to do whatever it takes to succeed. As Gene states, it allows them to sustain "their dedication to their efforts."

Now that they employ over 180 people, they no longer are able to sell directly to their clients. Running a company of this size will not allow that. But, this does not mean that Gene and Doug have stopped selling. Instead of selling their products directly to their customers, they are selling their sales philosophy to employees who deal directly with customers. Being street smart, their ideas have not changed since the early times. Sell according to customer needs, not only to generate the highest commission. Listen to what your customers have to say. Don't take your customers for granted; build relationships. This street smart philosophy will insure that Delson Business Systems, Inc., will remain a leader in its field.

8
The Presentation

What is a sales presentation? This is a simple, straightforward question, yet most salesmen are not able to answer it accurately. A presentation is the complete sales package that is given to a prospect for the sole purpose of getting him to commit to purchase a product or service. It is the road map that gets you from point A to point B. The world is full of underachievers who believe that their sales presentations begin the moment they first meet their prospects and end when they either get a "Yes, I will do business with you," or a "No, I am not interested."

Street smart salesmen know that this is nonsense. These tactical salesmen are aware that their presentations begin way before they ever meet their prospects. And when they do meet their prospects, they do not base their sales talk on a bunch of ad-libbed razzle dazzle. No way! These earners break down their presentations into component parts, and each part becomes an important element in making their sales calls successful.

The first element that goes into developing a successful presentation is preparation. Street smart salesmen learn as much as they can about their product, their competition, their customers, and their markets. As soon as the street smart salesmen become confident in this fact-finding process, they make sure that all their information is well organized so it can be used effectively. On many occasions, I have witnessed salesmen frantically looking for contracts, phone numbers, sales proposals, etc. Not very professional.

The sales pitch, the actual communication between you and your prospect, is the second essential element that goes into your presentation. During this time, you are trying to discover what your customer's needs are. This is accomplished by having a well-planned presentation that asks specific questions of your prospect, which, if your listening skills are where they should be, will supply you with valuable customer information. As soon as your prospect's needs are established, your presentation will indicate to your prospect how he will benefit, and satisfy these needs with use of your product or service.

At some point during your sales call, you are bound to encounter customer objections. This affords you the opportunity to prepare answers to your prospect's objections in a logical, straightforward, convincing manner.

The third component of your presentation should accomplish one of two things. It should indicate a decision on the part of your buyer to go or not to go with you, or a commitment for some future action such as a follow-up appointment.

The street smart salesman's roadmap is completed as soon as he is able to incorporate all these components into his sales presentation. Like a motorist on a journey, he will be guided from preparation to close by his sales presentation, directed how and where to go by the presentation's components. Meanwhile, he is free to anticipate any detours such as customer objections, questions, etc.

Underachievers are not successful because their presentations are poorly structured and ill-planned, which prohibits their picking up valuable clues and information necessary to successfully close their sales.

Presently, if on your sales calls you do not have a clear-cut understanding as to where you are going, it is time for you to develop a well-planned strategic presentation that will enable you to uncover the important clues in order to know just what your prospect's needs, wants, or interests are. Once that is accomplished, you will begin to make sale after sale. Read this chapter carefully; it will help you map out a money-making street smart sales presentation.

Preparation

Does a boxer go into a ring without getting into condition? No! Does a surgeon operate without years of study? No! Does an actor go on stage without any rehearsal? No! Does the street smart salesman go into a sales call without preparation? Absolutely not!

Like all champions, street smart salesmen prepare and practice their craft over and over again. They know there are no shortcuts to success. A salesman who goes on a sales call poorly prepared will severely cut down his chances to earn those large commission checks. Street smart salesmen will not allow this to happen, and neither should you.

This section will prove to be invaluable to you by helping you to prepare a well-planned presentation. Be street smart—start mapping out how and where you want to go; it will lead to big bucks!

❏ KNOW WHAT YOU'RE SELLING

Street smart salesmen want to know their products inside and out and then some. They are constantly trying to further educate themselves with new product information that will enable them to increase their product knowledge.

Underachievers believe that product knowledge means being familiar with a few features of their products or services, combined with having some buzz words to impress the prospect that they know what they are taking about. This is ridiculous.

You must be as familiar with your product as if it were part of your body. When you are explaining a feature of your product to your prospect, it is best to assume that he knows very little about your product or service. In most cases, your prospect will indicate to you if he is familiar with the point you are trying to make. Now that we have established the importance of product knowledge, I can see that you were just about to ask me what you should be looking to discover about your product or service. I'm glad you're eager to learn; let's get to it.

A good start in developing product knowledge is knowing the history of your product or service. If your company has made technical advances over the years, be able to talk about them in your presentation. Some of your sales might have been lost due to the fact that you were not aware of some of the achievements that your company has made over the years. These achievements could be in many different areas, such as manufacturing, packing, delivery, use of personnel, etc.

Perhaps your company started out in a small facility, such as a basement, etc. Indicate to your prospect just how far your company has come. Prospects like to do business with growth companies. It gives them a feeling of security, that your business will be around to service them in the future.

If your company happens to be second or third generation, tell your prospects that the owner has roots and cares about the day-to-day operation of his business. Emphasize that your boss is working extra hard to please his customers. He doesn't want anything to occur that will jeopardize a business started by his grandfather, grandmother, father, or mother. Talk about the values of past owners, and how these values were handed down from generation to generation. Sales talks that include these kinds of things help to promote trust, warmth, and rapport between you and your prospect.

In some instances, it might be beneficial for you to have a good understanding of what actually goes into the making of your product, especially if your company uses materials that go far beyond industry standards.

Where do you go if your company doesn't have this information readily available? This is another excellent question, and here is the answer. Talk to older employees; they often will tell you about the good old days when the company started in a little two-by-four office. A foreman in the factory can provide you with all sorts of information that can help you on your sales calls. Vendors who sell to your company can be an excellent source of information, informing you about the advances that they have made in the materials or procedures that they supply for your product. Other reps or salesmen can also give you a sense of company history. Try to locate old company brochures. Many times you can use them on a sales call, indicating to your prospect the many advances that your company has achieved over the years. Last, but not least, your boss can give you an excellent sense of history about the company. You will find that owners enjoy talking about their company's beginnings. The good old days, so to speak.

As a result of learning about new strengths of your products or services, you will be able to keep up a high level of enthusiasm. When you stop trying to learn about your products or services, you will tend to become bored and burnt out. It is impossible to excite prospects to buy when you yourself are unenthused.

By acquiring strong product knowledge, you as a salesman will develop the confidence needed to go after the larger and more difficult accounts. Underachievers are intimidated easily because they are not secure about what they are selling. They fear they will not have the knowledge to answer certain objections or questions.

Prospects can sense when a salesman is either nervous or unsure of himself, and prospects do not buy from salesmen who are unsure of what they are selling.

The more that you know about your products or services, the better you will be able to indicate to your prospects all the benefits that they can expect to receive by purchasing.

Someone once said, "Discovery is when you see something everyone else has seen and think of something no one else has thought of." That is exactly the way a street smart salesman looks upon his products or services, trying to come up with new insights that no one else has thought of.

Be street smart, do your homework, it will be well worth the effort.

❏ KNOWING YOUR COMPETITION

Street smart salesmen are aware that having strong product knowledge is only half the battle; the other half is gaining as much information about their competition as possible. These savvy salesmen would never develop a presentation that did not take into consideration who and what they are up against. Only then can they be in a position to construct a sales presentation that will be able to convey the strength of their products or services without knocking their competition. One of the worst things that a salesman can do is to overtly knock his competition. If you do such a thing, all it accomplishes is increased doubt in your customer's mind as to your own ethics, reliability, and the quality of your product or service.

In putting together their presentations, street smart salesmen try to get as much information as possible as to how and when their competitors will go about selling their products or services. If you are not aware, then you just might be selling at a tremendous disadvantage.

It is important to know if the people you are up against use give-aways, colorful brochures, consignments, etc. Common sense tells you that if you don't know, then how the heck can you plan a presentation that will beat your competition.

A good source of information is your prospects themselves. Your customer can specifically tell you what he likes or dislikes about the products or services he is using. In addition, some prospects will reveal if they are either satisfied or unhappy with the salesman who is presently servicing them. Often, they will even go into the reasons why they are happy or unhappy. You may learn that a salesman has become so confident about getting a prospect's business that he takes the prospect for granted. Instead of servicing the prospect face to face, he takes the impersonal route by using the telephone.

By doing some detective work, you will find out how often your competitor works his territory, and in some instances, you will learn the specific days that he visits his customers, which can be extremely helpful, especially if it is advantageous to you to be there first or last.

If it is possible, go out and buy your competitors' products. Read their brochures. If you're a service company, get your competitors' service contracts, guarantees, etc. See if you can unearth independent studies that will give you valuable information as to how your product or service does indeed stack up to your competition.

After you have compared and dissected your competitors' products, make a list of all the strengths and weaknesses that you perceive they have. Then make a list of all the strengths and weaknesses of your products or services, carefully analyzing how your products or services stack up against theirs. Without doing this exercise, you will never be able to arm yourself with enough information in order to handle product comparison, which I can assure you will be brought up by your prospects.

Be street smart—learn as much about your competitor as possible. If not, he just might take away the business you were counting on.

❏ SECURING REFERRAL LETTERS

A referral letter can be one of the most important items that you can have on your sales call. It indicates that a customer who has already used your product or service has not only been satisfied, but has been satisfied enough to sit down and write a letter recommending your product or service to others.

Amazingly, many salesmen are very lax or uncomfortable about asking their clients for these letters. Street smart salesmen realize that referral letters are too important not to be asked for. They know that in most cases, if a client is happy with your product or service, he will be willing to write you a letter of recommendation. The street smart salesman is not afraid to ask, because if a client is not happy enough to write him a letter, he wants to know the reason why. Many times, after he has straightened out a problem for a prospect, he then will be able to secure a recommendation letter.

The best time to ask for a referral letter is as soon as possible after your product or service has been used. At that point, your prospect will have the most enthusiasm for you, and your products or services.

In addition to getting your own letters of recommendation, ask other salesmen if they can share with you their letters that indicate client satisfaction with your products or services. The more testimony you have about your company, the more secure a prospect will be in purchasing your products or services.

Be street smart, get others to help you sell your wares. Remember, there is strength in numbers.

❏ RECORD KEEPING

Street smart salesmen know the importance of keeping good records. All their research involving product knowledge and competitors, as well as customer information, would not be worth very much if they forgot, misplaced, or simply did not bother to write down what they had discovered. Composing a presentation from memory leads to too many important omissions.

All the records of the street smart salesman are typed on index cards or paper and filed properly. Records that are filled with various kinds of scribble turn out to be of little value. Even worse, a misinterpreted thought can become a disaster when used during your sales presentation. Street smart salesmen do not want to waste valuable selling time searching for or deciphering materials.

In addition to being well-organized, these thorough salesmen know that it is just as important to have their records as complete as possible, allowing them to refer to any notes that might be helpful in preparing their presentation. Listed on the record cards, besides the usual data, are past conversations that you might have had with your prospect, as well as the reasons why you think you were not able to sell to him in the past. If your prospect has already bought, indicate on your cards what he purchased. You will notice in the example below that there is a place for customers' birthdays; use it. Whenever a prospect becomes a customer of mine, I ask him for his birthday. Many prospects inquisitively ask why, and here is my street smart answer:

> George, I send everyone in my family a birthday card. My clients are like family to me, and they get cards just like my kids, aunts and uncles, brothers and sisters.

Company Name   Ace Mechanical   **Date of appointment** 5/9/91

Address   1 Oak Drive   **City**   Roslyn   **State**   New York

Telephone   516-460-7890

Decision Makers   Thomas Miller and Gregory Smith

Comments Thomas seems to be in favor of going ahead with the project. Gregory does not seem to be as excited. They want samples of the insulating material.

Competition Morris Harvey seems to be the toughest competition. Their delivery, though, is only once a week, which might be the reason that they could go with us.

Follow Up Tom wants me to call at the end of April to confirm our appointment for May 9th.

Birthday   Tom 7/8/45   Greg 7/30/46

Referrals

Client Card

You may think this is corny, and it is, but it works. In addition to my card catalogue, I set up a monthly calendar listing all my clients' birthdays. The next time you are preparing to see an old client, look up his birthday. If it should happen that it is coming up shortly, congratulate him during your presentation. You will see how effective it will be in establishing rapport between the two of you.

An example of a client card is above. If there is any other pertinent information that you feel belongs in your records, include it. The more information that you have when going into a sales call, the better your chances of completing the sale.

Of course, you can establish your own record keeping system that conforms specifically to your own needs and style;

however, make sure that all your materials are located where they can easily be utilized.

Don't count on your memory for your record keeping—be organized, be street smart, leave nothing to chance.

❏ STAY IN TOUCH

There you are—at the right office, at the appropriate time—and the secretary says, "Sorry, but I called your office two hours ago to cancel today's appointment." Or, you make it back to your office at the end of the day and look down at your desk to see a note saying, "Call back hot prospect before 1 P.M.!!" Or, your secretary spots you coming in and tells you your biggest customer has left five messages for you to call him immediately, if not sooner. Bad timing? No. What we have here is a failure to communicate.

Every street smart salesman knows you have to make yourself accessible. If a customer needs to reschedule your appointment, if a hot lead comes in and needs immediate follow-up, if a question only you can answer needs to be addressed, you have to know. You have to make it your business—and that's what it amounts to—to be in direct contact with your office or your customers. Through the magic of electronics, we have all the technology we need to stay in touch: facsimile machines, mobile phones, answering machines, beepers, paging services, and pay phones. Each is designed to let the salesman know that someone wants him—and isn't it nice to know you're wanted?

By making sure your support people always know where to reach you, or by constantly calling your office, you will avoid the pitfalls of missed messages or, worse, missed opportunities.

❏ CLOTHES SELECTION

Street smart salesmen know the importance of dress, and they select their clothes very carefully before they go out on sales calls. They are aware that when a prospect decides to buy, his decision is based on the total package, and the salesman is part of that total package. Many sales have been lost because the image projected by a salesman's clothes has not been looked upon favorably by his prospect.

There is an old expression, "It is better to be overdressed then underdressed." For our male salesmen, I recommend that you always wear a shirt, a tie, and a suit. If you have to go on a job site with a client, you can always bring some protective clothing. Salesmen who wear casual clothes will not project the professional image that they want. Even if your prospect greets you in cut-off jeans, he will take notice of your professional look.

For salesmen, I recommend the following dress:

- *Black Socks.* Colored socks can be distracting. They do not project a professional image.

- *Navy Suit.* As you will learn later on, navy is a power color.

- *White Shirt.* White projects a clean-cut, honest image. Make sure that your shirt is wrinkle free.

- *Black Shoes.* As with colored socks, colored shoes can be very distracting.

- *Overcoat.* Cashmere is the best; wool is fine. Ski jackets and three-quarter coats do not project a successful, professional image.

- *Briefcase.* Leather is the only way to go. Vinyl, cloth, or supermarket bags are not acceptable.

Saleswomen have to be careful of the clothes that they wear, carefully trying to avoid any suggestion of sex. Women do have more leeway in the colors that they choose to incorporate into their clothes. They can wear prints as long as their clothes do not take away from the professional image that they are trying to establish.

For saleswomen, I recommend the following dress:

- *Suits*. Business suits indicate just that—you are there to do business. Navy and gray will give you that corporate image.

- *Skirt*. Choose a skirt that allows you to sit comfortably in front of a prospect, not having to be concerned with too much leg showing.

- *Blazer*. Coordinates well when wearing a skirt. It projects a nice corporate look. It indicates that you are there to do business.

- *Shoes*. Spiked heels are out. They do not convey a professional business image.

- *Handbags*. Handbags and briefcases should be leather; this will project that the person knows quality.

- *Jewelry*. Loads of jewelry takes away from you as the professional. Don't empty your jewelry box when you go out on a sales call.

- *Perfume*. Heavy perfume does not project the image that you want to give on your sales call.

For all salesmen, if your clothes look as if you have eaten too many chili dogs, bursting at the seams, bring them to a tailor; if the tailor can't fix them, buy a new suit. Remember, your hair and nails are part of the total package; it is essential that you be well-groomed.

Be street smart—keep them guessing, dress like a winner, even if you have only one outfit.

❏ YOUR SALES DELIVERY

Street smart salesmen understand that it is not always what you say to a client that makes a positive impression but, in many instances, how you make that statement. A salesman trying to convey his empathy to a client who is having difficulties will only hurt his chances of success if he does not convey a sincere feeling of compassion on his part. Prospects do not like to do business with salesmen who they feel are a bunch of phonies.

There will be situations during your presentation when you may have to express confidence, compassion, concern, etc., which will help you to develop a strong bond with your prospect.

In order to insure that your sales delivery conveys the messages that are needed, the following steps should be taken. If your sales call only requires you to give a talk, make certain that you script your speech before making it. By writing it down, you can then commit it to memory. Once it is memorized, you can practice and refine your presentation, creating the moods that are needed. You can show empathy, humor, or whatever other emotions are called for.

Speak in a confident tone, but be careful not to talk too fast, or you will give the impression that you are nervous. If you have to slow down, breathe deeply; it will help you relax.

I don't want to give you too much to remember, but you also have to concentrate on not speaking too slowly; this can give the impression that you are unsure of yourself, or even worse, that you believe your prospect is not smart enough to follow what you are saying. If you keep your enthusiasm up, you should not have any trouble.

If, on the other hand, you are going to demonstrate a product as well as give a talk, include a step-by-step analysis of what you are going to show off in your demonstration. Do a trial run for friends or colleagues. Ask them if you kept their interest up. There are very few things that are more boring then a poor demonstration.

A good practice exercise is to rehearse in front of a friend, relative, or colleague, having him role play as if he were a prospect. See if he can tell the moods that you are trying to convey. Ask him if what you are saying makes sense and is easily understood. Practice pacing yourself with clear crisp enunciation, changing pitch and tone every so often to avoid becoming too monotonous. Don't be afraid to be animated; use your arms to make significant points. Afterwards, have your listener as well as yourself critique your performance, making any additional changes that are required. Do this exercise over and over again until what you say feels and sounds completely natural and comfortable.

Underachievers who are not prepared, and put off practicing as if it is some kind of punishment, can sound awkward, stiff and confusing. Many times they even leave out important information that could be critical in making the sale.

As in other fields, champions in sales do not reach greatness without sacrifice and practice. Be street smart—practice, practice, practice; it will lead to commissions, commissions, commissions!

The Pitch

Your sales pitch, the actual face-to-face meeting with your prospect, is what all your work, preparation, and rehearsal was for. Street smart salesmen are keenly aware that this is their opportunity to make it happen. If you present yourself poorly the first time, the chances of getting another opportunity are slim. These superb salesmen know that if they perform in a professional, logical manner with a presentation that meets the needs of their prospect, their chances of earning those large commission checks are excellent, and that's the bottom line!

❏ THE FIRST IMPRESSION

Think about it. How long does it take you, when first meeting someone, to decide if you like that individual or not? I suspect not very long. At times, I don't even have to speak to a person before I can make the decision of whether I am going to like him or not. An arrogant gesture will turn me off sufficiently, after which I will try my best to avoid that person. On the other hand, I have found myself drawn towards an individual who merely displayed a nice warm smile.

Your prospects are also prone to making quick judgments

about you. It does not take them very long to make an impression as to what they think of you. Do not give them any help in formulating a negative one.

Walk in with confidence, head up, shoulders back with a warm smile on your face. Do not start out by making weak statements such as:

- "I won't be taking too much of your time."

- "Thank you for giving me some time today."

Many salesmen make the following typical, weak statement when their prospects either interrupt or stop their presentations to concentrate on some other matter:

"Take your time; I have all day."

Always be positive; remember you are there to help your prospect, you are an asset. Don't tell your prospect that you have all day. People who have all day do not have much to offer. You must make your prospect feel that you have an opportunity for him. Introduce yourself, your company, and your product in an upbeat, confident manner. Never apologize for being there. And for God's sake, be on time.

❏ NEED–SATISFACTION

Street smart salesmen are aware that their customers' needs are the focal point of any sales transaction. No one, and I mean no one, buys a product or service unless he thinks that it is going to satisfy one of his particular needs. Simply put, a *need* is something that your prospect wants. It can be a tangible item or an intangible desire.

You as a salesman must be able to communicate to your prospect how the benefits of your product or service will satisfy his needs. Your presentation has to be structured in such a fashion that it encourages your prospect to communicate to you what his needs are. And that is the key, having a two-way dialogue between you and your customer.

Knowing this, street smart salesmen have in their selling bags a list of probing questions that they can ask their prospects in order to gain valuable information about their needs, wants, or interests. These questions are prepared long before they even meet their prospect; they are built into the presentation. Even though most of the questions may never be used, they are still made available. In later chapters we will discuss in greater detail the importance of asking questions and listening to your prospect's answers. Below are examples of probing questions that can give you an idea as to how to discover customer needs:

- "What are the barriers that are preventing you from achieving great success?"

- "How is competition hurting you in the market place?"

- "If you were to retain a company like mine, what would you want it to do for you?"

- "What would you like to see as the future of your company?"

Pay careful attention to what and how your prospect answers your questions. A gesture, a tone of voice or whatever, can give you additional clues as to his needs. See chapter nine on "Subliminal Selling," which tells you what to look for and how to interpret your prospect's body language.

Be street smart—discover what your prospect's needs are; it will dramatically help you in satisfying yours!

❑ FEATURE–SATISFACTION

As soon as the street smart salesman establishes customer needs, he will indicate to his prospect all the unique features of his products or services that can satisfy his as well as his company's needs. A *feature* is any specific characteristic of your product or service that can be translated into benefits for your prospect.

In order for you to be able to translate the features of your products or services into customer benefits, it is essential that you have a thorough understanding of your products or services. That includes special achievements, unique manufacturing techniques, strengths, material advantages, and history of your products, services, and company.

It is critical that your presentation convey these unique features to your prospect so that he can truly see and understand how he will benefit by deciding to purchase your products or services.

Be street smart—know the important features of your products; it just might make you unique!

❏ BENEFIT—SATISFACTION

Street smart salesmen are aware that the key to selling is the process of satisfying customer needs with product benefits. A *benefit* is any perceived value of your products or services that can satisfy a prospect's needs. Product benefits are the link between your products' or services' features and your customer's needs.

Underachievers do not close their share of sales because they do not sufficiently indicate to their prospects how their products or services will benefit them. As a result, their prospects are not confident about making the decision to purchase. That is why many of the underachievers cannot overcome the "I want to think it over" objection. If their prospects were clearly shown how they could benefit from the underachievers' products or services, many of the "I want to think it over" prospects would purchase right away.

Be street smart—indicate clearly how your products or services will benefit your prospect. Once you do, you will reap the rewards.

❏ HOW TO USE NEED–, FEATURE–, AND BENEFIT–SATISFACTION SELLING

Street smart salesmen use need–, feature– and benefit–satisfaction selling to close a high percentage of their prospects. By using the technique of asking questions, they are able to uncover their prospects' needs. Once these needs are established, they are then able to indicate to their prospects all the unique features of their products or services that will benefit them as well as their companies. The following example will illustrate this point:

> *Customer:* I get a lot of returns due to widget corrosion. *(Need is established. A widget is needed that will not corrode)*
>
> *Salesman:* My widget has been specially treated with chrome plated latches. *(Chrome plated latches represent the special feature of the product.)*
>
> *Salesman:* As a result, you will no longer get returns due to widget corrosion. *(The customer will benefit by not getting any returns due to corrosion.)*

Be sure not to make the mistake upon hearing a customer need, of going right into closing and stating a benefit of your products or services without emphasizing any of the features. The following examples will illustrate this point:

> *Customer:* Sales are way down. I'm not making any money.
>
> *Salesman:* I can assure you that if you give our company a chance, you will make money.

By closing in this fashion, without using feature support of his statement, the salesman is asking his customer to take his word at face value. The correct way to indicate to his customer that he will benefit by his product would be:

> *Salesman:* Because our machine has a *Telflon Flibulator* (unique feature) it will produce your goods five times faster, which will dramatically cut your manufacturing costs. As a result you will be able to drop your prices, which will enable you to increase your sales. *(Customer benefit is established.)*

In summary, selling is the process of satisfying customer needs with product benefits. Your product benefits connect your product features and your customer needs. When a prospect feels trust and rapport with you, and perceives that your products or services will benefit him, he will most likely make a positive decision to purchase.

Be street smart—translate the features of your products or services into benefits for him; it will benefit you as well by meeting your large commission needs.

❏ ANTICIPATING OBJECTIONS

The third key component in your presentation is your ability to anticipate and handle your prospect's objections. No matter how thorough your presentation is, at some point your prospect is going to throw an objection out to you, and the way that you handle it can make the difference between making the sale or not.

The following exercise will help you anticipate what some of your prospect's objections might be. Thoroughly go over the presentation that you have written out. When you get to a point where you believe there might be a customer objection, write it down on a piece of paper. After this, do your presentation for a friend or colleague, asking him to give you any objections that might come into his mind. When you have finished these exercises, continue to practice and work on solutions to these problems. Practice your answers on your friends, getting additional input. You may not always be able to come up with answers that will satisfy all your customers, but at least you will sound professional and confident. The worst thing that you can do is to fumble for answers, which will only add to your prospect's concerns.

Be street smart—don't be caught off guard; try to anticipate as many of your prospect's objections as possible.

❑ OVERCOMING OBJECTIONS

The ability to anticipate objections is important, but not nearly as important as developing the skills to overcome your prospect's concerns. No matter how much you prepare and try to list everything that a client could possibly question, there will still be occasions when a prospect will throw out an objection that you did not think of.

Don't panic, the street smart salesman has everything under control. In chapter eleven, "Handling Objections," you will find means for overcoming client objections. These tactics will give you enormous confidence. No longer will you fear objections by your prospects; rather, you will welcome them. You will learn that customer objections indicate interest, and interest is all you should hope for when going on a sales call.

Be street smart—read and study the chapter on objections; it will help you overcome any of your concerns.

Closing

Closing is the last element in your presentation. It is the point when you ask your prospect for some action. Street smart salesmen are keenly aware that a strong presentation will give them an opportunity to ask their clients for commitment at different points during their sales talk. These proficient salesmen know that if they wait until the very end of their presentation to ask for the order, they are putting too much pressure on the decision-making capabilities of their clients. Street smart salesmen use trial closes in order to ask for the order at various times during their sales calls.

Trial closes give you an indication as to how positive or negative your prospect may be at certain points in your presentation. They allow you as a salesman to test the waters. A trial close gives you the flexibility to ask for the order without risking a halt to your presentation.

Many times a street smart salesman will trial close early in his presentation, often getting a "no." He simply states, "George, I get so excited talking about my product, sometimes I forget to give you all the pertinent information so you can make a positive decision, and that's just what I did with you. Of course you can't make a positive decision based on what I've told you." This allows our street smart salesman to continue his sales call. Notice how smart he was when he told his prospect that as soon as he gets all the relevant information he would then be able to make a positive decision. The beauty of the trial close is that your prospect most likely will tell you the definite reason why he is hesitant to purchase. This gives you an opportunity to concentrate your efforts on his concerns.

On the other hand, when you use a trial close, your prospect may give you every indication that he is ready to buy. If that be the case, forget the rest of your presentation and go right for the close.

An example of a trial close would be:

> George, when we start working with you, you will quickly see the difference in the way you are serviced.

After you have made this statement, the client might either give you a indication of agreement, or simply respond that he has not made up his mind just yet as to whether he is going to go with you. If you have used this trial close early in your presentation, you can the use the example that I gave you above to continue the sales call. He indeed needs more information before making a positive decision to go with you. On the other hand, if the trial close is used at the end and you do not get a "yes," simply ask "Gee George, what are the concerns that are holding you back from making a positive decision?" Wait for his answer. He most likely will give you the information that you need to use to try to overcome his concern.

In the chapter dealing with closing, you will find many additional tactics that you can use in order to get customer commitment. Study and incorporate them into your presentation. Role play with friends until you become comfortable and familiar with these techniques. The better you become at closing, the more sales and commissions you will make, which is the street smart bottom line!

Making Adjustments

Street smart salesmen know that part of being prepared is to expect the unexpected. These savvy salesmen understand that if they lose their composure or allow a prospect or situation to intimidate them, all chances for them to make a sale are most probably lost.

Read this section carefully and see how the street smart salesman handles some of these out-of-the-ordinary situations.

❑ SON-OF-A-BITCH PROSPECT

It is unfortunate when we come across a prospect who is rude, obnoxious, and arrogant, a real son-of-a-bitch. When a street smart salesman comes across this kind of client, he does not allow the client's actions to destroy his motivation or self-image. He realizes that he has not done or thought about doing something that warrants this type of behavior. Yes, he is there to make a sale, which in effect should also benefit his prospect. Neither he, nor any other salesman, is paid to take abuse. If a street smart salesman feels as if he is being abused, he handles it in this manner:

George, I sense by the way you are speaking to me that you do not like me. Did I do anything to offend you?

Most often, when you address a client in this direct manner, he will be taken by surprise. Like all bullies, when stood up to, he probably will back down and apologize for his behavior. On the other hand, if he looks at you and answers you in an abusive fashion, tell him in a nice way to stick it, that you think too much of yourself and your company to allow this to happen. You probably won't make the sale; but at least he will respect you. And more importantly, you will respect yourself.

Sometimes a son-of-a-bitch is not a son-of-a-bitch. He might tell you that you indeed said something that upset him. If his claims are legitimate, don't make excuses. Apologize; try to right the situation.

❏ TIME CUT DOWN

Just as you are about to begin your presentation, your prospect announces that, insead of an hour, he can only give you ten minutes. Don't make the mistake of trying to rush your sales call, hoping to be able to cover sufficient material in order to close the sale. More often than not, you will not have the time to make the impression needed.

Instead, inform your prospect that what you have to tell him is far too important to rush through. This gives him a sense of urgency to see you again. Tell him that you understand that emergencies come about, and that it would be far better to reschedule than not be able to give him the information that he needs. Not only have you given him urgency to see you again; but, in addition, you have also shown empathy for his situation. This helps to build rapport between the two of you. It can only help you the next time you see him. Remember, before you leave, make sure you get a new date and time for the appointment.

In this case, it is better to put off till tomorrow what you would have to rush through today!

❏ CONTINUED INTERRUPTIONS

There you are trying to give a professional presentation, and for the past ten minutes your sales call has constantly been interrupted by secretaries, phone calls, or what have you. As a result of this, you are finding it difficult to concentrate. And you are aware that if you are having problems concentrating, there is more than an excellent chance that your prospect is not grasping anything you are saying. Street smart salesmen know that if this is the case they have to stop their presentation and say:

> George, I know I cannot convey the importance of my product or service to you because I am finding it difficult to concentrate on the important points due to all the interruptions. Why don't we take a break so you can catch up on what you have to do; and then could you please hold your calls until we have finished. This way, you will be able to make a wise decision about my product or service.

If your prospect says it is impossible to hold back the interruptions, take this street smart approach:

Salesman: What time do you get into the office in the morning?

Prospect: 7 A.M.

Salesman: How about meeting me at 6:30, I'll bring the bagels and coffee, and we can talk in peace and quiet. (You can also use this tactic after hours if he is more of a night person. If he leaves the office at 6, meet him after closing.) I know you will benefit, because if we continue at this rate, you will not be able to get all the information that you need.

This approach shows that you care enough about him and his company to make the extra effort to come early or work late in order to accommodate him. Most prospects will appreciate this approach and agree to this arrangement.

❏ CLIENT ASKS YOU TO COMPROMISE YOUR PRINCIPLES

There might be times when you are asked to compromise your principles. It could come in the form of pay-offs to purchasing agents, or getting your hands on unrealistic amounts of samples in order to buy an order.

I can tell you that the business obtained through unethical practices is not worth the business. It will always come back to haunt you. A buyer whom you pay off owns you. And like the blackmailer who never gets enough, that buyer will continually up his demands, whereby it will become impossible to do business with him anyway.

If another prospect learns about certain favorable treatment, and he will, it most definitely will affect you with respect to getting his business. And who knows whom he will tell.

Inform your prospect that your as well as your company's reputation is everything. Ask him if he would be comfortable doing business with someone who is not trustworthy. Better yet, ask him how comfortable he would feel if he knew that someone working for him would compromise his company. Ease the tension by informing him that it would be your pleasure to have dinner with him or even take him to a show or sporting event. But you know that your company has made it a practice to give clients quality, service, and integrity, and isn't he happy that they have chosen to do that.

If he has an ounce of integrity, you will have made your point in a professional manner and should be able to get some business. On the other hand, if he doesn't have an ounce of integrity, you will get absolutely nothing. But be grateful; in the long run you will come out far ahead.

In summary, street smart salesmen are quick on their feet. They know that making adjustments is part of their presentation.

Advantages of a Well-Planned Presentation

Many salesmen avoid using a well-planned presentation because they are afraid that it will turn them into robots, making them sound stiff and void of personality. Street smart salesmen know that just ain't so; it's a total cop-out. The reason so many salesmen avoid a structured, well-planned presentation is due to the fact that they lack the discipline to develop one.

The fact of the matter is, a structured, well-planned presentation gives you greater flexibility than one that is based on ad-lib, off-the-cuff remarks. By thoroughly preparing yourself, you will be able to address and emphasize any area that your prospect might show interest in, not just the areas that you might feel most comfortable with.

If a prospect shows interest in long-term stability, you will be prepared to discuss how your products or services will provide him with long-term stability. If he shows interest in economy, you will be prepared to discuss how your products or services will provide him with added economy, and so on and so on.

By having a well-planned presentation, you will always feel that you are in control of the sales call; you will be secure in your facts, knowing exactly where you want to go. This helps you to develop enormous confidence in your abilities as a salesman, confidence that will help you make a favorable impression on your prospects. Prospects feel secure working with individuals who are confident; and when they feel secure, they buy!

A well-planned presentation insures that you will not forget to talk about important facets of your products or services.

Many times underachievers, because they conduct off-the-cuff sales calls, leave out pertinent information, which causes them to lose their sales. In addition, because much of their sales presentation is ad-lib, they tend to jump around, repeating facts that can become confusing to their prospects. Prospects do not buy when they are confused.

By having a well-planned presentation, street smart salesmen are able to concentrate on their prospects' thoughts and gestures. They do not have to worry about what their next thought should be. As we will discuss in further detail in later chapters, an important aspect of becoming a street smart salesman is to be able to pick up valuable clues from your prospects, such as gestures, tone of voice, etc., which will help you enormously on your sales calls. A salesman who has to concentrate on what he has to say cannot possibly pay full attention to the actions or thoughts of others.

Be street smart—don't get lost on your sales calls; develop a well-planned map. It will lead to much success.

In summary, street smart salesmen use well-planned presentations in order to turn shoppers into buyers. It helps them to discover their prospects' wants and needs. In addition, it helps them anticipate many of the objections that they might have to handle. Street smart salesmen, by being well prepared, know where they are going on their sales calls; they do not like to leave anything to chance. Be street smart—develop a well-planned presentation; it will keep you from getting lost!

The following questions are designed to help you develop a sales presentation that will work for you. Read these questions carefully and answer them either in your mind or on a sheet of paper.

1. Do you have a well-planned presentation?

2. If not, why not?

3. What are the strengths and weaknesses of your product?

4. What gains have your products or services made over the years?

5. Do you know who your competition is?

6. How do your products or services stack up to your competition's?

7. What are some of the implied unique strengths that you can allude to as special to your product or service?

8. What are some of the features of your product or service that you can use to satisfy customer needs?

You are now in a position to develop and implement a well-planned presentation. If at this point you still believe that sales is best done by an off-the-cuff, ad-libbing kind of approach then I am afraid that you will not be encountering the type of success that you are hoping for. If, on the other hand, you understand that sales is more then being a fast talker, then you have taken a large step towards becoming a street smart salesman.

Roberta Kane

Roberta Kane is an extremely successful street smart recruiter, earning fabulous commissions for the better part of seven years.

Success did not come easily to Roberta. She entered the job market in her forties, having been a housewife all of her adult life. Roberta quickly discovered that being a housewife was a handicap, not an asset, when she started looking for a job. Employers wanted people with experience and were not particularly interested in the fact that she had successfully raised two children. The only positions that she was offered were entry level, with limited earning potential. Roberta was not interested in these jobs; she was street smart, Roberta wanted more. She wanted the opportunity to achieve greatness.

The recruiting profession gave her that opportunity. It was the perfect vehicle for a street smart individual like Roberta. Since her compensation was based solely on her own performance, rather than being a guaranteed weekly salary, Roberta understood that her earning potential was virtually unlimited. In addition, being a recruiter allowed her to operate as if she were in her own business. This way, she was able to fully utilize her enormous motivation, perseverance, and creativity.

Roberta was aware that her success was dependent on two factors, getting client company job orders and filling these orders with the best possible applicants.

As a street smart recruiter, she knew that it was extremely important to know who her clients were. She kept street smart records. Roberta not only was able to greet her customers by their first names, but she could ask them about their families and about any stories that they had previously discussed with her. Being street smart, she knew the importance of building relationships. She asked questions and listened carefully to her customers' responses so that she would understand just what their needs were.

Instead of sending a large number of applicants to be interviewed, hoping to fill a job order, Roberta would overscreen, insuring to the best of her ability that her clients would not be wasting their time interviewing a candidate that she recommended. She worked street smart, to her clients needs, never compromising in order to gain a commission. As a result of bonds that she has developed with them, her customers look out for her. Often they recommend her services to others.

Roberta understands that it can be a difficult time for individuals who are looking for a job. Knowing this, she spends a great deal of time relaxing her clients, informing them of what to expect when they go on a particular job interview. As a result, her applicants are usually well prepared before they leave her office.

Roberta is aware that the key to her success is obtaining job orders from her client companies and filling them with the best possible applicants. Being street smart, she is constantly networking, talking about her services to friends, relatives, and people with whom she does business. Roberta always stays in touch with old clients, never allowing them to forget their recruiter. She also stays in contact with individuals that she has placed, networking to see if they know of any qualified people who might be looking for a position.

Roberta states, "My business is an extension of my life. I always think about my business and how I can improve upon it. It is not because I am a workaholic. It is because my business has been good to me, allowing me to enjoy life to the fullest. I want to protect what I have built up." I guess you can say that Roberta has the right street smart attitude.

9
Subliminal Selling

There is a point during street smart salesmen's presentations when their prospects seemingly develop an instant trust and rapport with these dexterous salesmen that at times makes it appear as if the prospects purchase without any overwhelming reason. This is due to the fact that street smart salesmen have developed subliminal selling skills, enabling them to influence their prospects subconsciously.

I know what you are thinking, I'm getting a little too carried away with the abilities of these street smart salesmen, now making them out to be some weird mind-controlling products pushers. That's not the case; street smart salesmen are not witch doctors using their voodoo skills to make sales. What they are using is psychological, body language, and observational techniques in order to gain a valuable selling edge.

If you want to become a street smart subliminal salesman, positively influencing your prospects on a level they are not aware of, put your Doubting Thomas's views in your back pocket and read this chapter carefully. I will teach you the skills necessary to develop a strong bond between you and your prospect. And remember, prospects buy from salesmen they like and believe in.

Observation

Street smart salesmen are aware that one of their greatest sales tools is their sense of observation. These savvy salesmen make many a sale because they have picked up valuable clues, through observation, that often give them a better understanding as to the interests and wants of their prospects.

Knowing the importance of observation, they are like sponges soaking up everything around them, looking for that one clue that will give them the insight necessary to positively influence the prospects in their favor. These perceptive salesmen know that a prospect's desk or walls can scream out with information that can be invaluable.

By carefully reading this section, you will discover some of the things that street smart salesmen look for in order to make a connection with their prospects. Once you understand the hidden subtleties behind these clues, it will become easier for you to communicate with your prospects, which is essential if you are going to be a successful salesperson.

☐ CLASSIFYING YOUR CUSTOMER TYPE

As individuals, we all have unique thought patterns that are influenced by our own environment and interests. Think how helpful it would be for you as a salesman to have an understanding of how your prospect thinks. How often do you try to communicate with one of your customers and just don't connect. Many times you write it off as either you're having a bad day, or your customer is being just a disagreeable so-and-so. The problem is, if you don't know how to zero in on your prospect's thought processes, you will have to rely on the old hit-or-miss method of connecting, which unfortunately leads to many, many days that you want to write off.

Be street smart; stop guessing how your prospect thinks. Read and study this information carefully; it will help you to think and communicate as your client does.

A fascinating study conducted by Richard Bandler and John Grinder, psychological researchers, led to the conclusion that individuals' thought processes can be influenced by the way information is presented; that is, they either see, hear, or feel what you are saying. They call this neuro-linguistic programming or NLP. They go on to say that prospects fall into three distinct groups, either visual (lookers), auditory (hearers), or kinesthetic (feelers), according to the way they respond to information and language. Once a salesman has the ability to discover which group his prospect falls into, he then is able to direct his presentation to the level that would most influence his prospect to purchase.

The Lookers

Visual prospects are individuals who respond positively to images such as brochures, colorful pictures, and creative language.

Street smart salesmen, when they are selling in front of a visual prospect, consciously use language that will allow their customers to vividly picture the benefits of the product or service they are being sold. Simply put, it is faster and easier for a visual to understand what you are trying to say as long as he can see your ideas in his mind.

An underachiever, not aware of these three distinct groups of prospects, has no idea to whom he is selling; and if he is lucky enough to build trust and rapport, it is due to chance more then anything else. An underachiever will have enormous difficulty selling to visual prospects if he is using language that inhibits his customers from creating these visual images.

What are the key characteristics to look for in order to discover if you are indeed selling to a visual prospect? That's a good question and one that I knew you were going to ask.

When speaking to a visual prospect, you will observe that his eyes move rapidly. This is due to the fact that he is actively trying to picture in his mind exactly what you are saying.

Another clue to determine a visual prospect is his use of

language. Visual individuals tend to use words that create picture images such as *view, show, bright, picture,* etc. Some typical visual sentences would be:

- "Can you *show* it to me?"
- "That's a really *bright* concept."
- "I can *see* what you mean."
- "That's awesome, I can really *picture* that in my mind.
- "I have a slightly different *view.*"

A street smart salesman knowing that he is selling to a visual prospect, will employ the following subliminal selling tactics in order to create strong rapport:

> George, can't you *see* that magnificent car in your drive-way. Believe me, I can just *picture* you cruising down the highway. Your friends are going to go crazy when you *show* them that car.

By the time this street smart salesman has completed his sales presentation, his prospect, on a subconscious level, will not only be able to vividly picture himself driving the car, much to his satisfaction, but he will also feel a bond towards this creative salesman, making it much easier for him to make a decision to purchase.

Be street smart—when with a visual prospect, sell what he can see; it will help you create those big bucks!

Listeners

The second group of prospects described by Bandler and Grinder are auditories. These individuals respond most favorably to the way you deliver your information. It is not so much what you say, but more importantly, how you say it through your pitch or tone. These factors have a lot to do with developing rapport with auditory prospects.

Auditories use language that conveys a feeling of sound, such as:

- "George, that *sounds* great to me."

- "I'll *call* you next week to discuss it."

- "Go to your room, don't use that *tone* with me."

- Believe me, I *hear* what you are trying to say."

Auditories frequently will put their hands on their face, as if that will assist them with their hearing.

Auditories are not as verbal as visual prospects, since they are thinking over in their mind decisions that they are contemplating making. Over and over again they will verbalize to themselves the pros and cons of the decision.

Back to our street smart car salesman. Now that he realizes that his prospect is not visual, but is instead auditory, he makes the necessary changes in his presentation to reflect the differences, flexible enough to still be able to develop a strong bond with his customer.

> George, when you start up that engine it will be *music* to your *ears*. At seventy miles an hour that car is as *quiet* as a mouse. When you kick it into fourth gear that motor just begins to *sizzle*.

Be street smart—practice these tactics so you will be comfortable using them with auditory prospects. When selling to these types of individuals, use language that builds rapport between the two of you. If you do, when you ask him to purchase, his response will be music to your ears!

Feelers

The last category of prospects are kinesthetics. These individuals base their decisions more on how they feel than on what they see or hear. They are more emotional and make decisions more from the heart than from the head.

Not surprisingly, kinesthetics' vocabulary consists of words like *touch, grab, hold, feel*. Some typical kinesthetic statements would be:

- "George, I know how you *feel*."
- "I *felt* the same way myself."
- "Tell me how you *feel* about that."
- I can *appreciate* that myself."

Kinesthetics are "feely" people. They like to hold your products in their hand if possible. You will see them touching samples, brochures, etc. At times they will also reach out to touch you in order to make a point; they are more animated when they speak than the other two groups.

Again we shall return to our street smart car salesman, this time using subliminal tactics that relate to kinesthetic individuals.

George, just *feel* that leather, isn't it fantastic? Only when you drive down an open highway can you fully *appreciate* how dynamic this car is. All my clients *feel* like teenagers again, especially when *their hair blows* in the wind.

Be street smart—get these types of customers to feel what you want them to buy; it will touch your heart in the right spot, by making you big bucks!

Now that you are aware of these subtle differences between individuals, the next time you are on a sales call, use your skills of observation to try to discover which category your prospect falls into. It will allow you to establish strong rapport with your prospects that undoubtedly will lead to increased sales, which is the street smart bottom line!

☐ ELEMENTARY DEDUCTION

The old saying, "A picture is worth a thousand words," holds true for our street smart salesman. When he enters a prospect's office, he quickly scans the walls looking for any kind of clue that can help him gain insight into his prospect, making mental notes of what he has seen so they can be used when needed in his presentation.

From experience, a street smart salesman knows that pictures, plaques, or awards tell a great deal about his prospect.

Often a client will have pictures that will indicate if he is a sports or hobby enthusiast. There might be a picture of him jogging, playing golf, fishing, running trains, etc. Many top executives, as a result of the pressures of running a company, find sports and hobbies a wonderful outlet for their frustrations and enjoy talking about them. Street smart salesmen are aware of this and read up on many different hobbies and sports, just so they will have some information in their bag of selling skills to enable them to ask a question or simply to small talk, all of which goes a long way in building up rapport. Nothing breaks the ice better than asking a prospect about his favorite activity.

If your prospect enjoys an adventurous activity such as flying, this might be a indication that he is not afraid of taking chances with a new product or service. In addition, individuals who take part in activities that could be somewhat dangerous are usually good decision makers and like you, as a salesman, to get right to the point. They don't want to dilly dally or hear a lot of bull.

Photographs can indicate if your prospect is a family man and could reveal if there might be another generation coming into the business, which could be especially helpful to you as a salesman if you are selling a product or service that offers growth, security, and financial stability. After all, as good parents, we certainly do not want to bring our children into a company that will have problems in the future. Street smart salesmen selling consulting services, pension plans, etc. find this information useful.

A plaque, award, or picture can indicate a favorite charity, service, club, or organization that he might serve in for his community. The street smart salesman uses this bit of information to build rapport by either discussing the various causes or by playing on his prospect's ego by mentioning how much he respects him for getting involved in such a worthy cause. Done in the right manner, this can be extremely beneficial for you on your sales call.

You may come across a client who has a designer showcase for an office with absolutely no personal momentos. This could indicate that your prospect has strong feelings about the way things appear.

There are literally hundreds of things to see. Through experience and practice you will be able to discover clues that could make the difference between making the sale or not. Be street smart, look for the clues; it's elementary, my fellow salesmen!

❏ DESK MANAGEMENT

There is an old adage, "If a messy desk is a sign of a messy mind, what does an empty desk indicate?" The answer to that question is dependent upon whom you speak with. The problem is that there are many interpretations. Psychologists themselves do not agree on what a cluttered or empty desk means with respect to a person's make-up. However, I have my own theories.

Upon entering an office that appears to be outwardly well-run, with a high level of success, noticing an executive with a messy desk in this setting would indicate to me that this individual has a hands-on approach in his management style. In addition, many executives with cluttered desks have strong egos, not really overly concerned with their personal image. These prospects are ususaly easier to communicate with, allowing you to be fairly informal in your sales approach.

If, on the other hand, the office gives you the impression that the business is only marginal, or the office does not seem to be well-run, an executive with a messy desk in this scenario just might be overburdened. Seeing this, you should set up your presentation by being empathetic and indicating to your prospect that using your product or service will help to relieve some of his pressures. If you have to leave various materials behind, such as proposals or brochures, make sure that there is something visible on your paper work that will allow it to stand out so it will not be lost in his sea of other paper work.

A clean desk may indicate that your prospect is someone who does not like to be viewed as a person who does not take care of business immediately, especially if it might not be true.

These executives very often are image conscious, and therefore your presentation should reflect this fact by appearing professional, organized, and knowledgeable.

Be street smart—pay attention to your prospect's desk; it could help you clean up.

Psychological Subliminal Selling

As a result of using certain psychological techniques, street smart salesmen are able to develop a real selling edge. These techniques are so subtle that their prospects for the most part are not aware that they are being influenced by them.

Many of these techniques have been used to influence you to make various day-to-day decisions, either through television, magazine, radio, or newspaper advertising. Did you ever wonder why you buy a certain cereal, drink a certain soda, etc.? Advertisers have been aware of these tactics for years; now you have an opportunity to learn them also. Be street smart, read this section carefully; it's a psychologically sound idea!

❏ TRIGGER WORDS

In October of 1983, Yale researchers reported that there are certain key words that trigger a positive response in individuals. These findings were published by the National Association of Life Underwriters.

Advertisers are so aware of these trigger words that they tend to overuse them. It seems like every year a particular product is *new* or *improved*.

Street smart salesmen use these trigger words as much as possible in their day-to-day selling, via the telephone, their sales calls, or in their correspondence materials.

The study disclosed what they felt were the twelve most influential words to your customers' ears. By using these words, you will better be able to establish rapport and trust with your prospect.

The following list of twelve words will prove to be invaluable to you. These are the words that the researchers found provoked positive responses in individuals. Read, study, and use them on your sales calls. They will help you to influence your prospect on a subliminal level in your favor.

1. *Discover.* People like to be part of a new discovery. The proof of the pudding: Sears Financial Services chose to name their new credit card "Discover," which was brought out to compete head to head with Master Card, Visa, and American Express.

2. *Easy.* Prospects like to be able to purchase with ease; they are tired of the day-to-day complexities of life.

3. *Guarantee.* People are afraid to be cheated; they react positively to products or services that offer guarantees.

4. *Health.* Health is the most important thing to individuals, and that includes money. As a prospect gets older, health becomes more precious.

5. *Love.* Everybody reacts uniquely to the word; it is the most emotional word in our vocabulary.

6. *Money.* Everybody wants it, and I mean everybody. Even the rich can't get enough of it.

7. *New.* If it's new, we assume it just has to be better.

8. *Proven.* Proven gives the impression that something is

tried and true; it just plain works. People want things they can depend on.

9. *Results.* Results convey a positive bottom line image. "This product gives results." People like that; it makes them feel that they will be getting what they paid for.

10. *Safety.* Products that are safe conjure up trust and reliability, features that prospects want.

11. *Save.* Everybody enjoys a savings, either in dollars or time.

12. *You.* Using the word *you* personalizes your approach, making your prospect feel as if he were special. People like to feel special.

Practice using these words. If *you* do, *you* will *discover* how *easy* it is to influence your prospects, *saving* you precious time trying to convince them that your products are indeed *safe, healthy,* and *proven* to produce the *results* promised. If *you* do, I *guarantee* that you will *love* how well your prospects will respond.

Be street smart, use these techniques; it will lead to big money.

☐ SUBLIMINAL COMMANDS

The street smart salesman uses subliminal commands to assure his prospects that they are doing the right thing by deciding to purchase.

The technique is simple; in order to get his prospects to remember important aspects of his presentation, the street smart salesman will emphasize certain words or phrases in a statement that will reinforce as well as draw attention back to a point or benefit of his product or service.

* "George, *you will benefit* from this program just the way all my other clients who have *purchased.*"

- "When you *own* this car it will make you feel young again."

- "I know this product *will work for you.*"

- "Based on what you've said, I know you will *gain enormous satisfaction.*"

A subliminal command can also be effective if you use a phrase that a prospect seems to favor. If a prospect frequently says, *"This is the greatest thing since sliced bread,"* to indicate that something is special, you can take this statement and use it as a subliminal command.

George, this program is the *greatest thing since sliced bread;* you are going to enjoy it.

Be street smart, practice using this subliminal technique; *I know you will be successful.*

☐ TACTICAL IMPLIED SELLING

The street smart salesman, by phrasing a statement in a certain way, can subliminally influence his prospects to assume that his products or services have unique strengths. These artful salesmen are then able to create an image in their prospects' minds that they are dealing with a company that has special qualities. Individuals like to do business with companies that have special qualities. The following statement made by a clever street smart home improvement salesman will illustrate this point:

The people who will be installing your windows, Mr. Brown, *work only for us. We do not sub-contract our work.* This enables us to control the quality of installation, insuring that you will have no problems in the future.

By making a statement such as the above, the street smart salesman is allowing his client to assume that employing one's own installation employees is unique to the industry. This may or may not be the case. What is important is that the client perceives it as a benefit.

Consider all the areas of strength that you might be able to use to your advantage when speaking to a potential customer. Areas of possible unique strengths that you can look to include in your presentation are:

- People
- Product
- Inventory
- Delivery

- Client Base
- Service
- Experience
- Reputation

Include these unique strengths to your advantage in your presentation; it's the street smart thing to do!

❏ COLOR POWER

The street smart salesman is aware of how color can affect his prospects and, as a result, he uses it on a subliminal level in order to influence his customers in his favor.

If you doubt the power of color, which car do you perceive goes faster, a red or brown Corvette? The majority of people absolutely believe the red one. Advertisers have long understood the power of color. When you are looking through a magazine, see how often red is used when trying to convey speed. On the other hand, if an advertiser is trying to get across an image of invincibility, you will see the color brown displayed prominently. A brown eighteen-wheeler is a heck of a lot sturdier than a pink one, isn't it?

Knowing this, the street smart salesman incorporates color into his presentation on a subliminal level in order to gain trust and rapport between himself and his prospect. After reading this, you may decide that it is time to throw out a few of your business clothes, finally realizing that they just weren't the right fit!

Studies have indicated that there are three colors that clearly have a positive subliminal effect on an individual. The colors blue, dove gray, and hunter green will create an image of leadership, stability, security, and success. These colors should make it into your presentation either by your dress or support materials:

- *Blue.* People associate stability and leadership with the color blue, which is the reason why so many politicians choose to wear blue suits. The next time you are watching a debate on television, just look at how many of the candidates look as if they purchased their clothes off the same rack! Companies that spend money on brochures would be wise to incorporate blue throughout, especially in their logo. Visual prospects respond well to salesmen who wear blue suits.

- *Dove Gray.* Dove gray creates an image of stability and security in an individual's mind. If you are not sure that this is true, think about the color of security trucks, as well as the fact that most airport terminals are painted dove gray. A tie of dove gray is a nice subliminal touch with a blue suit.

- *Hunter Green.* They have found that people associate this color with money. Using this color in brochures for companies that are selling investments can be extremely effective.

The studies also have found that the three worst colors are black, which people associate with death; purple, associated with sickness; and yellow, associated with high anxiety. In fact, they discovered that the color yellow actually was able to increase anxiety and blood pressure levels in a short period of time. In addition, people over fifty found yellow to be the most irritating color to the retina.

Now that you know the power of color, use it to your advantage with your prospects. You will find it especially effective with your visual clients.

Be street smart—let blue, dove gray, and hunter green find their way into your clothes and support materials; it will lead to hunter green big bucks!

Body Language

Street smart salesmen have known for a long time that a great deal of communication can go on without anyone uttering a sound. Body language often says a great deal more than the spoken word. A raised eyebrow, a slouch of a shoulder, and a nod of a head are examples of how individuals can send meaningful signals to each other, and in many instances people are not aware that they are sending them.

In this section, you will learn how to interpret your prospect's body language, as well as how you can use your own body language to your advantage on your sales calls. Be street smart, read this section carefully; understand how the unspoken word can be mightier than the sword!

❏ HAND SHAKES

For most of us, a handshake is simply a greeting between two people, but not for our street smart salesman. A handshake offers valuable clues, clues that just might tell him a little bit more about his prospect, which could help in successfully completing a sale. The following handshakes will describe to you just how much you can actually learn about an individual without having him utter a single word:

- *Firm Handshake.* A firm handshake indicates that your prospect is a tough, bottom-line person. He will not be easily intimidated, and you'd better have the facts to back up your statements.

- *Upper Handshake.* This unique style of handshake whereby an individual places his hand in a horizontal position on top of yours, squeezing it in a vise-like fashion, is a strong indication that you will not be talking to anyone closely resembling Mr. Rogers, or anybody in his neighborhood. These individuals can be tough and abrasive, and have a definite need to always remain in control. Can you say the word "Intimidating?" You as a salesman cannot allow yourself to be intimidated, losing all control of your sales call, for if you do, your chances of successfully completing a sale are slim. If during your sales call a prospect is rude or abrasive, it is best for you to stop your presentation and address the problem by saying:

George, I don't understand why you seem to be so annoyed with my being here. If I said anything to offend you I apologize; believe me, I am here to help you, I am on your side. Are you just having a bad day?

or

George, I have come here with the best of intentions, yet I feel hostility on your part towards me. What seems to be bothering you?

Wait for his response; it will surprise you. By making this kind of direct statement, confronting someone's poor manners, you will most likely catch him off guard and he often will either apologize or discuss what is concerning him, which may have absolutely nothing to do with you. This approach will help you regain control of the sales call, frequently putting your prospect on the defensive. Most individuals do not intentionally want to be rude. More importantly, this will help you keep your own self-respect; nobody should allow himself to be abused.

- *Dead Fish Handshake.* This kind of handshake may indicate that your prospect is nervous or unsure of himself. Keeping that in mind, the street smart salesman uses a lot of empathy on this sales call, constantly reassuring his prospect that he is making a wise decision to purchase. Individuals displaying this type of personality might need some added pressure in order to make a decision.

- *No Handshake at All.* Not a great sign. This prospect probably regrets the day that he agreed to see you. Knowing this, the street smart salesman tries to pick up any additional clues in order to try to break the ice by talking about something that is close to his client's heart, such as sports, his family, or his favorite charity.

❏ EYE TALKING

The street smart salesman is aware that a lot can be learned through his prospect's eyes.

A customer who blinks in rhythmic beats or deliberately looks away from you is sending you the message that he was not really receptive to what you just said in your sales presentation. At that point it is essential for you to clarify your point with him in order to try to get agreement. Go over the information, then look sincerely into his eyes and ask, "George, you look as if you have some concerns over what I just said; what are they?" Listen for his response. After you have clarified your point, he may indicate that he has no concerns, or he may tell you that he feels what you have said holds no water; and if that's the case, at least you now know what objection you will have to overcome in order to make the sale.

Prospects who are in deep thought, considering what you are saying generally have their eyes focused on a stationary object. They do this, as opposed to looking at you, because they do not want to be interrupted. Let your prospect think, even if you have to pull out some paper work, pretending to do some figuring. When he wants to resume the sales call, he will turn his head back to you, which is a signal to move on. You might ask, "George, you look like you were in deep thought; is there anything you want to share or question?" Often he will let you in on what he was thinking, which can help you enormously in completing a successful sales call.

When a prospect continually looks away from you while he is talking, and all the while his eyes are moving from side to side as if they are watching a ping-pong game, there is an excellent chance that this prospect is lying to you. The only thing that you can do is to make one of the following statements:

- "George, are you absolutely sure about your facts?"

- "Gee, George, I've been in the business a long time and I've never heard that one; are you sure?"

- "You're going away for a week; let's set another appointment for a day after you come back."

Frequently a prospect will know that you have caught him in a lie, and, by making a statement like the above, you give him an opportunity to get out of his lie.

The street smart salesman can use his eyes to convey many, many moods, such as empathy, enthusiasm, sorrow, and confidence. When shaking hands with prospects, he looks straight into their eyes with a nice big smile that indicates confidence in himself. When the sales call is over, even if it was not successful, he does the same thing, never leaving with his head or eyes down, which would convey the feeling of defeat.

If a street smart salesman wants to give his prospect his best power stare, indicating that he is one tough confident cookie, he slightly closes his eyes, slowly moving them from side to side, concentrating not to blink. This kind of look can be very intimidating to the person you are staring at.

Using your eyes to convey different moods takes practice. By using a mirror you can practice using your eyes to express different frames of mind, such as joy, anger, sorrow, etc. After a while, practice with friends by having them guess the feeling you are trying to express.

Be street smart—listen to what your prospect's eyes are telling you; it could help you see those large commission checks!

❏ GESTURES

Prospects make statements through slight movements of their bodies, which can give you valuable insight as to how or what they are thinking. For this reason, street smart salesmen look intently for that frown, shrug, or what-have-you in order to pick up a clue that can help them to successfully complete a sale. Underachievers rarely pick up any of this information, which severely limits their ability to achieve.

If, during your sales presentation, you observe your prospect shaking his head in agreement with what you are saying, it might be in your best interest to ask for the order.

On the other hand, a prospect who has a frown on his forehead, all the while rubbing his chin, is sending you a message that he has some concerns, concerns that must be addressed promptly or there will be no chance for a sale. At this point, look deeply into your prospect's eyes, opening your eyes wide to give you a Bambi-like appearance that conveys sincerity, and ask, "George, I get the feeling that there is something bothering you, what is it?" Many times, as a result of your eyes expressing sincere concern, the prospect will tell you exactly what is on his mind, which should help you enormously in successfully completing that sales call.

Prospects show disinterest or boredom either by pretending to pick off particles from their clothing or by rubbing their eyes and forehead. The message is clear: they can't wait for you to leave their office. If you see that your prospect is about to go into a coma, change your tone of voice, become more animated with your hands, and immediately direct some questions to him that just might stir up some interest on his part.

> George, I'm doing all the talking, let me ask you a question. What would you like to see happen if you engaged a company like my own?

Wait for his response, get him to talk; even if he expresses that he doesn't have much interest, at least he is getting involved. Once you know his feelings and concerns, you have a starting point to work on.

A prospect who subtly rubs the side of his nose with his fingers, occasionally forcing a cough that is as phony as Ed McMahon's laugh on *The Tonight Show,* and at the same time covers his lips with two or three fingers, is telling you that he is skeptical. If you see this occurring, pause briefly, conveying the feeling of thought on your part, and ask:

> George, I get extremely excited talking about my prod-
> uct/service and at times my prospects interpret my en-
> thusiasm as an exaggeration on my part about how they
> will benefit from my product/service. Do you think that
> I have been exaggerating?

The fantastic thing about this approach is that your prospect
will tell you if he believes you have exaggerated, which gives
you an opportunity to deal with this objection and, if done
successfully, to make a sale.

Street smart salesmen use body language in order to send
messages to their customers. If used properly, body language
can indicate that they are confident and enthused about what
they are doing.

These apt salesmen know that if they sit in front of a prospect
with little movement, stiff as a board, it will send the message
to their prospects that they are nervous and unsure of themselves.

When a street smart salesman wishes to make an emphatic
point, he will put his fingers together while raising his hand in
the air. Moving it in this manner gives the impression that he is
chopping wood. John F. Kennedy, our late President, used this
technique very effectively. If your prospect is not following
your chopping motion with his eyes, it indicates that his mind
is someplace else; and, if you are going to make the sale, you
had better bring it back.

An individual who talks with a limp wrist conveys the feeling to his prospect that he is weak. A stiff wrist, clenched fist,
and strong upper arm movement will cure you of this problem.

Be street smart—listen carefully to your prospect's body language; he is trying to tell you what's on his mind.

❏ MIRRORING

An excellent subliminal tactic employed by the street smart
salesman is a technique called mirroring. Studies have found
that it is possible to develop high rapport with clients through

nonverbal mimicking of their body actions. If a prospect crosses his legs, you cross your legs; if a prospect puts his hands to his face, you put your hands to your face. The street smart salesman does this in such a subtle manner that his prospect is not aware that he is being mimicked. Nevertheless, this tactic helps to establish fantastic rapport, making it much easier for these savvy salesmen to successfully complete their sales.

How many times have you been on a sales call when your prospect has been ill at ease, rude, or simply not that interested in what you had to say. By using this tactic, you can develop rapport that will relax your prospect as well as gain his interest in what you are saying, which is essential to your success. It will amaze you how it will disarm even the toughest of clients.

Be street smart; don't be too heavy-handed about mirroring. Do it subtly and see how you can improve your rapport with clients, making your sales calls go much more smoothly!

Developing Your Subliminal Techniques

Observational, psychological, and body language techniques are not exact sciences that can guarantee you perfect results. What they give you is an edge, an opportunity to send and gather information that can be helpful to you during a sales call.

These skills, like any other skills, have to be developed; and, until they are, you will not be able to pick up all the valuable information that is available to you.

The more you try to incorporate subliminal psychological tactics, such as trigger words, etc., into your sales presentation, the better and more comfortable you will be in utilizing this technique. The same holds true with respect to body language. To master these techniques, you have to practice the basic skills. Start off slowly, using the mirroring technique. Concentrate on your prospect's eyes, gestures, etc. You will be surprised how much it will help you on your sales calls.

Your observational skills also have to be developed. After all, it would be impossible for me to give you all the variables that could come about through observation. Only through experience and practice will you be able to pick up and use these clues to your advantage. The following exercise will help you to develop a keen sense of observation.

Pick a room in your house and walk into it for ten seconds. Then go in another room and write down everything that you observed, trying to be as specific as possible. Then return to the room and see what you left out. Go to different rooms of your house each day and use this exercise. When you are finished going through each room of your house, start observing your closets, by opening them for about five seconds.

While at work, observe how your fellow workers walk, talk, dress, shake hands, manage their desks, etc. Go into friends' offices and quickly look around, writing down all the things that you saw. Go back and see what you might have missed.

In a short period of time, this exercise will help you develop a keen sense of observation, wherein it will become second nature for you to pick up on most of your prospect's subtle, but important, nuances. Be street smart—become the sponge and clean up, by making those big sales!

The following questions are designed to get you to begin to use these subliminal tactics during your day-to-day sales calls. Read these questions carefully and answer them either in your mind or on a sheet of paper.

1. Presently, do you use observation to help you during your sales calls?

2. Specifically, what changes would you have to make in your current presentation in order to use the subliminal tactics on visual, auditory, and kinesthetic individuals?

3. Generally, what colors are your business clothes made up of?

4. Would you find it difficult using the mirroring tactic?

5. If so, why so?

6. Specifically, what tactics would you use in order to incorporate the twelve trigger words into your presentation?

7. When you walk into a prospect's office, what are some of the things that you look for?

8. What do you look for in your prospect's body language that could help you during your sales call?

9. Presently, are you using body language as a sales tactic?

10. If not, why not?

I know even at this point that there are still a few Doubting Thomases out there who do not believe in the effectiveness of subliminal selling. That's fine as long as you are willing to give it a try. If you are not, you then will be allowing yourself to lose out on a valuable selling skill.

The individuals who believe now have the information necessary to influence prospects on a level that they are not aware of. Practice these tactics; once you have gained the experience to plant positive seeds in your customer's head, you then have taken a major step towards becoming a street smart salesman.

10
Tactics for Overcoming Fear

In chapter four, "Like What You See," I stated that a key element necessary for the street smart salesman to achieve greatness is to have a positive self-image. I pointed out how there are two variables, one internal and the other external, that influence the development of a person's self-esteem.

The internal factors are directly related to the way an individual perceives himself, as well as the way he believes others see him. The external factors have to do with your surrounding environment, such as your job. Depending on the way an individual sees himself, internal and external factors can either be translated into positive or negative behavior.

Street smart salesmen translate these internal and external factors into positive behavior. They will not allow their fears, anxieties, or poor self-image to get the better of them. They realize that if they allowed this to happen, they would not be able to function at their highest level, and they refuse to accept that!

Read this chapter carefully. Learn to develop the techniques that will teach you how to confront your problems, deal with them, and overcome them; it's the street smart thing to do.

Taught to Fear

For the most part, the factors that cause us fear, anxiety, and low self-esteem are taught to us by others. These lessons are well learned and keep many of us from performing at our highest level. We are conditioned not to try to achieve greatness. A parent who, with all the best intentions, tells his child to take a particular job, curriculum, etc. because it will be easy, safe, and secure, is really telling his child that the child does not have what it takes to achieve greatness. We are conditioned to stay away from certain courses, professions, accounts, etc. because others have told us that they are too difficult, that we would not be able to succeed. Unfortunately, many of us are listening to underachievers, to individuals who were too scared to take action in their own life necessary to achieve greatness.

Why do you think so many children are scared to death of dogs? Certainly, we are not born with the fear of dogs, nor for that matter of any other animals. It's because parents have done an excellent job of telling their children that if they get too close to one of these mongrels, they just might get one of their hands bitten off.

I had a dog who was so old that he could hardly see or hear. On top of this, he was in dire need of dentures. Nevertheless, every time my cousin came over to my house and my dog just happened to wander into his path, he would go totally bezerk, as if he were about to be eaten alive. My aunt did one helluva job of instilling the fear of dogs in my cousin.

When a parent screams at a baby to stay away from a hot stove, that child immediately develops a fear of that stove. In some instances, not knowing exactly what to be afraid of, the child can transfer that fear to other related objects such as a pot or a pan.

When we are children, our peers can negatively influence how we feel about ourselves. Everybody wants to be socially accepted and liked. When we become the butt of others' cruel jokes or comments, we tend to withdraw, and we develop a poor self-image. The many individuals who base their self-esteem on others soon end up miserable, frustrated, and depressed.

As we get older, we see how we might become afraid under certain circumstances, especially by subconsciously accepting others' fears as our own. A statement such as, "I'm scared to death speaking in front of people," is an example of how a negative thought of others can influence the way we think and react. That is one of the reasons why so many individuals have problems speaking in front of groups.

From early on we are conditioned to fear change. That is why so many people use the word "no" as if it were an involuntary response to being asked to make a decision. Think about it; when you go into a clothing store and a salesperson comes up to you and says, "Can I help you?" what is your first response— "No, I'm just looking." "No" insures that the status quo will remain. Individuals who are afraid of change limit their chances to achieve greatness because of their lack of confidence in themselves. They are prisoners of their own self-destructive insecurities.

In many instances, individual fears can appear to make little sense. People on one hand can be terrified to speak in front of a class, yet amazingly enough have no fear of sky diving. Nevertheless, no matter how nonsensical fears might be, they are still real to the individuals who experience them. Fears can lead to feelings of inferiority, shyness, and extreme anxiety.

Individuals who have inferiority complexes are basically fearful people who see themselves as inferior, constantly putting themselves down by verbalizing their own self-defeat, rejection, and low self-esteem. When you feel inferior, having a low self-esteem, you truly are afraid to face life, with all its highs and lows. People who feel inferior use language such as, "I could never do that," "That's beyond me," or "I'm just an ordinary Joe."

Fears can be so terrible that you can develop anxiety and apprehensions about things that may or may not happen. People can't sleep at night because they have anxiety about the possibility of being audited. Salesmen start to sweat profusely because they fear that a prospect may have a complaint or a question that they might not know how to answer.

Street smart salesmen understand that if fears, anxieties, and poor self-esteem are learned, they can also be unlearned. Read, study, and learn to unlearn everything that's keeping you from achieving at the highest level.

Identifying Your Fears and Anxieties

Street smart salesmen are willing to confront their fears and anxieties head on. They are aware that this is the only way that they will be able to overcome them. It may involve forcing themselves to solicit on the telephone, or confronting their bosses regarding a particular concern.

Street smart salesmen are keenly aware that if they did not confront their problems, and instead played it close to the vest, they would miss out on enormous amounts of opportunities and happiness in life. The individual who is terrified to ask a girl for a date misses out on all the pleasures associated with dating. The salesman who is afraid to solicit the large accounts will never have the opportunity of achieving those large commission checks.

Before you can confront and overcome a fear or anxiety, you have to be able to identify it. That is the only way you can truly understand what you are up against. The street smart tactic that you will use is to make a list of all your fears and anxieties. For this to be effective, you have to include as much detail as possible, such as people, situations, or thoughts that are causing you to have anxiety. It is important for you to describe how these fears and anxieties are affecting you emotionally and mentally. Lastly, include a history of your fears and anxieties, starting with your earliest recollections and ending with your last experience. Below is an example of how this should look on your piece of paper:

FEAR

1. *Talking to a group.* Whenever I have to make a presentation, I become irritable and unable to sleep, and I develop stomach cramps. The first time I can remember feeling this way was when I had to make a speech about Abraham Lincoln in front of my fifth grade class. Last week I had to make a

presentation to a group of buyers, and the same old feeling came out.

2. *Making a decision.* I become nervous and clammy every time I have to make a decision. The first time I can remember feeling lousy about making a decision was when I was trading some baseball cards with some friends and I heard someone say that I was a jerk. Last month I walked out of a car showroom because I became so uncomfortable about making a decision regarding which color I should choose.

Now that you have identified what your fears or anxieties are, you will be able to concentrate on overcoming them. Read the next section carefully; it will provide you with the street smart tactics necessary to deal with your problems and concerns.

❑ THE TACTIC OF VISUALIZATION

Once a street smart salesman identifies his problems, one of the techniques that he uses to overcome them is called visualization.

Visualization is a process whereby the street smart salesman pictures in his mind an upcoming event that normally would cause him to have fear or anxiety. Instead of allowing this image in his mind to cause him discomfort, the street smart salesman learns to visualize himself responding in a confident, positive manner, which helps to eliminate his fear and anxiety.

Daydreaming is a form of visualization. When your daydreams are positive, they help you relax. The positive commands that your daydreams send to your brain keep you happy and alert, which enables you to achieve at a higher level than you normally can.

The day before a big game, professional athletes often dream about the game, vividly picturing themselves performing a particular feat. They find that this helps them to mentally prepare themselves.

Just like the professional athlete, you are going to create positive visualizations that will mentally prepare you to overcome your fears or anxieties. Let's suppose one of the events that causes you a great deal of anxiety is when you have to make a presentation in front of a large account. Close your eyes, and start picturing this scenario in your mind. You are greeted with a warm smile by your prospect, who gives you every reason to believe that he is happy to see you. As you are going through your presentation, you are handling all of his questions and objections in a logical, convincing manner, much to the satisfaction of your customer. Finally, picture yourself shaking your prospect's hand, walking out with the signed contract.

In order for visualization to work, you have to follow some simple rules. Most importantly, your visualization always has to be positive. It will only create more discomfort if you allow negative images to enter your mind. If you visualize a prospect who is rude and obnoxious, you will experience even more anxiety before that sales call.

Also, the more detailed your visualizations are, the more effective they will become. See yourself writing up your sales contract. Picture that smile on your prospect's face. Imagine how happy you are putting that signed contract in your attaché case. Look carefully; you're smiling.

Finally, practice this technique. The more you use it, the more effective visualization will be for you.

Give this technique a chance; it works. You will see that any situation that causes you to have fear or anxiety can be overcome through visualization by creating a positive solution of that event. Be street smart—picture yourself a winner; it will help you overcome many obstacles.

❑ THE TACTIC OF AFFIRMATION

Many people are their own worst enemies, by unwittingly putting themselves down. They plainly don't like themselves.

Street smart salesmen avoid doing this by using the technique of affirmation. Affirmative statements are positive commands that you give to yourself in order to keep your motivation level high. This technique is essential, for unless you make a real effort to do this, negative thoughts will eventually creep into your mind, causing you to become depressed and frustrated, all the while feeling poorly about yourself.

For individuals who suffer from anxiety, the following affirmations should be used frequently:

- "I am a good person, I deserve success."

- "I am good. In fact, it's frightening how good I am."

- "Nothing is going to stop me from succeeding; I have the ability to achieve greatness."

An excellent technique for people who don't feel positive is to wake up in the morning and say, "It's great to be alive." When you first look into that mirror, you must see yourself as a winner, able to achieve greatness. "I like you, you're going to do great things today. Nobody, and I mean nobody, is going to stop you from becoming a champion."

At the end of each day, write down all the positive things that took place. Even if there was a setback, write down what you learned from the experience, turning a negative situation into a positive one. If, for example, you do not make a sale the first time, you then would say, "I learned a lot from this sales call, I'll get him the next time"; and when you do, you'll say, "I am good!"

When they close a sale, street smart salesmen unconsciously say to themselves, "I am good." They are not blowing their own horns or trying to put someone else down by telling themselves how good they are; what they are doing is confirming their belief in themselves through positive affirmations.

In order to get the most out of this technique, follow these rules:

Make your affirmations as specific as possible. If you have problems giving group presentations, simply say, "I have everything under control. I know my demonstration is going to go very well."

Affirmations should always be positively worded commands. If you say, "I am not scared of this presentation," the use of the word *scared* conveys a negative feeling. Instead you should phrase your affirmation in this manner, "I am confident and prepared to make an excellent presentation."

Reinforce your affirmations with positive visualizations. If you see yourself acting with confidence, back this image up with affirmative commands.

Street smart salesmen would be the first to tell you that everybody has setbacks. But by seeing yourself as a winner, continually talking in positive terms to yourself, you will be able to keep your spirits and motivation high enough to achieve great success. Be street smart, talk positively to yourself; it will make you perform better.

❑ OVERCOMING THE FEAR OF TALKING

A common fear among individuals is a fear of talking in front of a group. Even though salesmen earn their living by talking, often they are not comfortable speaking either to a large account or in a group situation, especially when they have to make demonstrations. Because speaking to an important account or group is so essential to your success, I am treating this particular fear as a separate topic, giving you additional insight as to how to overcome it.

As previously discussed, you can use the tactics of visualization and affirmation to help overcome this particular fear. By visualizing yourself making a strong, confident presentation and combining it with affirmative statements such as, "I know I sound confident," you will go a long way towards solving this problem.

In addition to visualization and affirmation techniques, whether you know it or not, there are a host of other things that you can do to overcome this fear.

There are courses in public speaking that are offered at your local community centers, high schools, or colleges. There are courses given by private self-help companies such as Dale Carnegie, which will provide you with helpful hints in public speaking.

The Phobia Society of America is a nationwide group of therapists, doctors, and recovering phobics who give all sorts of valuable information as to how to deal with your problem. Willard Scott, the weatherman on the *Today* show, is a member of this organization.

There are many books that you can read that can help you deal with this fear, such as: *Breaking Through* by Julian Asher Miller, *Anxiety and Panic Attacks* by Robert Handly and Pauline Ness, and *Not to Worry* by Mary McClure Goulding and Robert L. Goulding.

As you should do with any kind of activity that you are uncomfortable with, sit down and critique your performance after practicing it, noting the changes that will improve it. Then go through the process over again, asking your friends or relatives to see if there was any improvement. Go through this process over and over again until you feel that you have conquered the fear of communicating; it's the street smart thing to do!

❏ REWARDS AND PUNISHMENTS TACTICS

Whenever a street smart salesman forces himself to make a significant effort to overcome something that causes him anxiety, he rewards himself with something special. It could be a new camera, clothes, etc. The important thing is that he knows that he deserves this special prize for trying, no matter if he is successful or not.

On the other hand, if he procrastinates and just doesn't put in the effort to try to perform, he gives himself a punishment. It might be cleaning out his closets, washing his car, or sitting in on a weekend.

Be street smart—do what you have to, then reward yourself for a job well tried.

❑ RELAXATION TACTICS

It is extremely important for you to learn how to relax. Individuals who are always tense have a difficult time identifying as well as solving any of their problems.

It is not unusual for people who are nervous, tense, or feeling highly anxious to start to breathe rapidly, which causes them to get dizzy, which causes them to become even more upset and scared. The dizziness comes from the increased oxygen that enters the blood stream as a result of rapid breathing. Obviously, it becomes virtually impossible for individuals to solve any of their problems under these conditions.

When a street smart salesman experiences these feelings, he goes through one of his relaxation techniques in order to get himself to calm down.

If you feel sudden anxiety before a sales presentation, try this exercise. Close your eyes and take a deep breath, all the while tightening every muscle in your body. Stay in this position for approximately six to eight seconds, then let your breath out. At that point, with your eyes still closed, breathe in a rhythmic pattern for twenty seconds. Repeat this routine three times; by the end, you should feel more relaxed, allowing you to deal with your anxiety.

When you are feeling fatigued and tense at the end of the day, try this method to relax. For twenty minutes or so, with your eyes closed, focus all your attention on one word or a fixed point in your mind. The greater your ability to focus your mind on the word or point the more relaxed you will become.

Lastly, listening to soft easy music can be very relaxing. The street smart salesman always has a few of these tapes in his car in order to clear his head before his next appointment.

Be street smart, practice these techniques; a salesman who is tense will invariably make his prospect tense. And customers who are tense do not buy!

❏ ARE YOU TALKING TO ME?

Street smart salesmen work very hard at keeping up a positive, upbeat attitude. They are aware that if they are going to achieve greatness, it is essential that they remain motivated.

They use the techniques of visualization—seeing themselves as winners—and affirmation—telling themselves they are winners—in order to keep themselves positive.

In addition to these techniques, they know the importance of associating themselves with individuals who are winners and have a good attitude about life.

It can be extremely stimulating and motivating when you are in the company of people with high aspirations. If you need a push or a boast, invariably you will be able to get it from these types of individuals. By being with positive people, you tend to reinforce your positive thinking.

As we learned in chapter four, negative people can help destroy an individual's self-image and motivation. Because of this, street smart salesmen stay away from these types of individuals as if they have the plague, and in a way they do, for they are carriers of self-destruction.

The tactic a street smart salesman uses if he happens to find himself trapped in the company of a negative person is simply to tell him to stop being so negative. At times, individuals are so down and depressed that they are not aware that they are being so negative, and they occasionally will thank you for your honesty.

If you notice that the people you are hanging around are still negative and won't change their attitude, remember, you have the option to make new friends.

The next time you hear someone trying to contaminate your thinking, be street smart and leave, and I mean leave!

❏ USE WHAT'S OUT THERE

Self-help material is used by the street smart salesman to reinforce all his positive thoughts.

There are self-help books just like the one you are reading right this second that can give you invaluable insight and information. Books like *Never Be Nervous Again* by Dorothy Sarnoff and Gaylen Moore and *Making What You Say Pay Off* by Edward J. Hegarty will give you valuable information on public speaking. Go to your local library and seek out the books that will help.

There are self-help cassettes just like the street smart salesman cassettes that you can listen to while driving in your car. Zig Ziglar and Tom Tompkins have produced excellent motivational tapes. Cassettes are useful since they allow you to zero in on the areas that you find most interesting and important.

There are a variety of public speaking courses available. Some are offered through local community centers and high schools. By making a few phone calls, you can learn where these local courses are given.

There are also private organizations on public speaking, such as the Dale Carnegie Institute. If you open up your local phone book, you should have no problem finding them.

If you discover that you need professional help, don't be afraid or embarrassed to go for it.

Be street smart, investigate all the self-help avenues that are out there for you; they just might offer you the support needed to achieve the greatness you are after.

In summary, street smart salesmen use these tactics for overcoming fear to gain control over their lives. They are aware that it would be impossible for them to perform at their highest level if their minds were constantly preoccupied with doom and gloom.

Be street smart; practice these tactics and remember what Franklin D. Roosevelt said, "The only thing you have to fear is fear itself."

The following questions are designed for you to better understand and practice these techniques. Relax long enough to read these questions carefully, and answer them either in your mind or on a sheet of paper.

1. Make a list describing all your fears and anxieties.

2. Go through each of the above and use the techniques of visualization and affirmation in order to help you deal with these concerns.

3. Do you like yourself?

4. If not, why not?

5. If you did an inventory of the people who surround you, such as friends, relatives, or fellow workers, would you classify them as being negative or positive?

6. What would you like to give yourself as a reward for a job well done?

7. What are some of the methods that you are presently using to relax?

8. Do you find that your mind is constantly preoccupied with negative thoughts?

9. If so, why so?

You now have learned the tactics used by the street smart salesmen for overcoming their fears, anxieties, and frustrations. If one does not work for you, you now have the ability to try another. Street smart salesmen know that it is impossible to eliminate all their fears; and if you, too, understand this and are able to deal with your fears on a level that still allows you to achieve positive things, then you have taken a large step towards becoming a street smart salesman! In addition, the skills found in this chapter go beyond selling. Learning to like yourself will not only reflect upon the way you feel but will also have a profound affect on who you are as a person and the way you interact with family and friends. It's only street smart to go for it!

Stanley Kushner

Ten years ago, Stanley Kushner sold his company, Sun Dew, to Dellwood Foods, Inc., a large dairy operating out of New York. Since the sale, Stanley has stayed on as president of Sun Dew. Stanley is one successful street smart sales executive.

Sun Dew was started by Stanley's father over fifty years ago. Fresh out of college, Stanley joined his father in business. Stanley said his dad was ecstatic that his son was going to work side by side with him. After all, his dad's dream was that his son was going to take over for him one day and send his checks to Florida, where he would lounge in the sun. Unfortunately for Stanley, his sales training consisted of his dad buying him a new suit and pen, with which he was supposed to write lots of orders.

Two days after his dad bought him his new suit, Stanley was called into his dad's office. His father instructed him to go see their largest account. He told Stanley that the account seemed to be unhappy about a price increase. His father said that they were reasonable people, and all Stanley had to do was show them that the increase was due to the rise in sugar prices. Seemed easy enough. Off Stanley went with his new suit, pen, and invoice indicating the increase in sugar prices.

For almost an hour, he sat in the reception room waiting to see their unhappy client. Finally, he was escorted into the executive's office. The following story was told to me by Stanley. He swore that this was the most humiliating experience of his life. The executive was indeed unhappy. When he saw Stanley, he became outraged. He started cursing and screaming at Stanley with his dissatisfaction that Stanley's father had not taken the time to come to see him. "What's the matter, your father has become such a big shot that he no longer has time to see good customers like me?" He was so infuriated that he jumped up from his chair and grabbed Stanley by his new suit jacket. Puffing his enormous cigar in Stanley's face, he went on with his cursing and screaming. When Stanley handed him the invoice indicating the price increase, he merely ripped it up and threw it at Stanley. At this point, Stanley was devastated, and was perspiring as if a sudden case of malaria had taken over his body. The following words were the only thing that Stanley was able to get out. "Mr. _____, you are frightening me to death. Please give me a break. It's only my second day on the job and already I'm going to cause my dad to go out of business." Stanley said that he must have been a pathetic sight and that the client must have taken pity on him. The client calmed down and listened to the reason for the price increase. Stanley stumbled through by telling him that his father was anxious for Stanley to meet his favorite customer. Stanley was not sure if the client had bought his story, but at least he stopped yelling and cursing at him and agreed to pay half the increase.

Being street smart, Stanley made an important decision that day. He never wanted to be put in that position again. He knew he needed to know a great deal more about his father's business before going out on sales.

The first thing he did was tell his father that his new suit for the time being belonged in the closet. He wanted to start from the bottom, which was the factory. And Stanley did just that. For almost two years, he worked in the factory. By the time he entered sales, he knew the inner and outer workings of the manufacturing process. He understood the formulas that made up drinks, and could intelligently explain to customers the advantages of purchasing Sun Dew.

When he officially became a salesman, Stanley continued his street smart ways. He drove in the delivery trucks visiting all his accounts, insuring that Sun Dew received the best placement in the stores. He spoke to every store manager and owner, introducing himself. He listened to their recommendations and complaints, making the changes that were necessary. Through the years, he continued his practice of visiting accounts, even though the majority of the orders were telephoned in. Because of the street smart way that he built relationships, Stanley developed for Sun Dew the largest market share among independently owned grocers. To this day, he still visits the accounts that he had as a young man. They know they can count on Stanley and that he has not forgotten them.

Stanley Kushner also has not forgotten the lesson that he

learned a long time ago. Know your product, know your market, know your customer, be prepared. That is what he teaches and preaches to the people in his company. Stanley is a street smart salesman.

11
Handling Objections

An objection is a point made by a prospect that stops him from making a positive decision to purchase. How you handle your prospect's objections can make the difference between making the sale or not.

Inexperienced salesmen as well as underachievers fear customer objections because they do not have the skills to handle them. They lack the understanding as to why customers will use objections before they will commit to purchase, no matter how badly the customers want a product or service.

On the other hand, if you look closely into the eyes of a street smart salesman right after he hears a client's objection to buy, you undoubtedly will notice a star-like glimmer. This glimmer is there not because he's crazy. Believe me, these savvy salesmen are crazy like a fox. But that glimmer is there because he knows that objections can end up being his best friend on a sales call.

The street smart salesman understands that when a prospect voices an objection, it is a signal that there is interest. That prospect is crying out for help and support. What he is saying is, "I'm not sold yet, but if you can convince me on this point I might be." That is all a street smart salesman asks, to be in front of a prospect with interest. He knows it is his job to overcome any objections that his client might have. And these expert salesmen work hard in developing their skills to handle customer concerns.

If you have a prospect who is constantly nodding his head in agreement, never voicing an objection, don't start planning on spending that commission check just yet. You could be in deep trouble. Often, there is little interest when a prospect is nodding in agreement with every point that you are making. Many times what he is acually thinking to himself is, "When is this guy going to be finished. Why did I agree to this appointment." Finally, when you ask him to purchase, his nod changes to a shake of his head, which emphatically indicates that there is no way that he is ever going to buy from you. Underachievers become discouraged and depressed. After all, they thought that sale was like money in the bank, only it turned out to be a bounced dream!

If you do not presently get a glimmer in your eyes when you hear a prospect's objections to purchase, then it is time that you develop the street smart skills to handle objections. Be street smart, read and study this chapter carefully; it will teach you how to turn your prospect's objections into your best friend!

Why Prospects Object

Did you ever wonder why an individual would object to purchase, when he gave all indications that he really wanted and needed your product or service? Often, not having a valid objection, these individuals will come up with all kinds of ridiculous excuses not to buy. Do you believe these kinds of prospects enjoy giving salesmen a hard time by throwing barriers and obstacles into your path, trying to hamper your efforts to sell them?

Some prospects do enjoy giving a salesman a hard time. But more often than not, this is not the case. It is more of a state of mind as to why individuals choose to make up all sorts of excuses not to buy. The better you understand their reasoning, the easier it will be for you to overcome their objections in order to successfully complete the sale.

❏ ONE—THE PANICKY BUYER

Many individuals find making a decision a very difficult task. I have an aunt who practically has a nervous breakdown every time she has to make a decision, and I mean any decision. I bought a house faster than it takes her to decide if she is going to have Cheerios or Rice Krispies for breakfast.

There are a lot of people just like my aunt. When they are faced with a situation that calls for a decision, they will begin to perspire as though they were sitting in the middle of a desert. Many times these individuals will blink incessantly and avoid eye contact. If they should happen to be with someone else when they are asked to make a decision, they will constantly ask their companion, "What do you think?"

When selling to these types of individuals, it is even more essential that they feel a strong bond with you than your typical prospect. These individuals must believe that you are out for their best interests. They have to be constantly reassured of this fact. This can be accomplished by making statements that indicate empathy on your part, such as: "I know how you feel, I have felt the same way myself." By doing this, you will make them feel more secure in doing business with you. And that's the street smart bottom line.

❏ TWO—THE UNBELIEVING BUYER

You may find this hard to believe, but some people do not trust salesmen. Prospects are constantly keeping their guards up trying not to be cheated.

Knowing this, you have to pay careful attention to what your prospect is saying. This will insure that you will be able to satisfactorily answer any of the objections that he might bring up. You must never slide over or avoid addressing a prospect's questions or objections. You might believe that you are real slick by avoiding some of his objections, thinking that your prospect has forgotten what he had asked you. Take this advice to the bank, prospects do not forget anything. When you don't answer his objections or questions, your prospect feels that you are trying to hide something from him. If you don't know the answer to one of your prospect's questions, tell him you don't. The worst thing that you can do is make up some story that is pure bull. Upon hearing some cockamamie story, a prospect will shut you off faster than you can say, "No sale." There is nothing to be ashamed or embarrassed about for not knowing an answer to a customer's question. Tell him it's a great question. Build up his ego. Reassure him that you will get back to him with the proper information. He will respect your honesty.

In order to build up trust, street smart salesmen will repeat a prospect's thoughts and answers. This indicates to your customer that you are paying complete attention to him. You are concerned with what he is saying. Customers are so used to salesmen talking full blast that they immediately respond positively to this approach, which helps to build trust and rapport.

Think before you respond to one of your prospect's questions. Too quick an answer indicates that you don't think too much of the question, or even more important, that you don't think too much of the person asking the question.

After answering an objection, make sure before moving on in your presentation that you have answered his question to his satisfaction.

> George, it's important for me to answer all my clients' questions to their satisfaction. Have I answered all your questions to your satisfaction?

If your prospect indicates that you have indeed answered his question or objection, then you have taken a major step in building trust between the two of you. Prospects buy from salesmen whom they trust.

On the other hand, if your prospect indicates that you haven't answered all his questions to his liking, ask him specifically what was not answered.

> George, I'm sorry I didn't answer all your questions. Tell me which one I missed and what additional information you need to know.

Be street smart—answer all your prospect's questions and objections; if you don't know the answers, admit it, it is the street smart thing to do!

❏ THREE—I'M NOT AN EASY MARK

Individuals throw out objections even when they know deep down that they are going to buy. They do this because they do not want to look like an easy mark to their salesman, friends, colleagues, family, etc.

Think about it. Very often, when you speak to people who have made purchases, they will say that they bought the best and at the lowest price. Ironically, many times individuals will boastfully say this even when they know that they have gotten ripped off. People just don't like to admit that they have been taken; they want to save face.

In addition, people will throw obstacles into your path because they don't want to hear it from a boss, colleague, friend, wife, or even worse a mother- and father-in-law that they were a chump, a salesman's dream. And if they had gone shopping with any of the above, they most certainly would have gotten a much better deal.

Prospects who feel this way will come up with all sorts of ridiculous excuses not to buy, testing your patience to the limit. Do not become too frustrated or discouraged. Hear them out. Answer all their objections, no matter how nonsensical they may sound. In many instances, after they feel that they have put up sufficient buyer resistance, they will turn around and do what they always wanted to do in the first place, buy your product or service.

❑ FOUR—PROSPECTS NEED TO KNOW

Many times prospects object simply because they were not supplied with enough information to buy.

Undreachievers who do not listen carefully to their prospects rarely discover what their customers' needs, wants, interests, or concerns are; and, as a result, underachievers are not able to supply their customers with enough meaningful information that will indicate the benefits of purchasing their products or services.

A well-planned presentation can help you avoid this problem. Underachievers who do not have well-planned presentations often will omit important information, which can be confusing to their prospects. And when prospects are confused, they will offer all sorts of opposition to purchase.

Be street smart—give your prospect all the information that he needs to purchase, and do it in a manner that he understands.

Rules for Handling Objections

There are basic rules that you must follow if you are going to successfully answer a prospect's objections. Follow these rules carefully and I will guarantee you that you will be cashing those large commission checks, which can be very rewarding.

❑ DON'T ASSUME ANYTHING

Street smart salesmen do not assume what their prospects might be trying to say. If a prospect makes a statement and they are not absolutely sure what he means, these savvy salesmen are smart enough to ask for more information. Salesmen lose more sales by making wrong assumptions as to what their prospects are trying to convey.

- "George, for my own edification, are you making this purchase for an investment or pleasure?"

- "Mr. Jones, I'm not entirely sure what you mean by your statement; could you please give me more information."

Remember, you do not want to spend your time justifying or struggling to answer an objection that does not exist in your customer's mind. Even worse, by wrongly assuming what your prospect is interested in, there is a good chance that you might be ignoring points that are truly important to him, which will surely cost you the sale.

Be street smart—if you are not sure what your prospect has in mind, ask him to restate his question, clarifying the points that you are not sure of. Don't assume anything; if you do, you might as well assume that you are not going to make the sale!

❏ DON'T WIN THE BATTLE AND LOSE THE WAR!

Salesmen who argue with their clients do not remain in sales very long. Even if you know for certain that your prospect is dead wrong about an issue, you still should avoid getting into a confrontation with him. If you do, it will be the surest way of killing any of your chances of making a sale.

In order to try to overcome an obstinate prospect, street smart salesmen will use third party stories. Third party stories are excellent for handling these kinds of obstinate individuals. They allow you to make a point without backing these individuals into a corner. You are able to illustrate how somebody else suffered dire consequences simply because they did not listen to reason and preferred to continue doing things their own way. The following example will illustrate how effective a third party story can be in this situation:

George, about three months ago I was with a client much like yourself, who also believed that upgrading his system was a waste of money. Even though it was against my better judgment, I went along with his thinking, although I knew I should have given him a lot more pressure to convert over. George, I didn't want him to think that I was trying to sell him something that he didn't need. To make a long story short, because he refused to upgrade, he had a total breakdown, costing him thousands of extra dollars, not including all the downtime that he experienced. Looking back, I sincerely wish that I had given him more pressure; I'd hate to see that happen to you.

By using a third party story such as this one, you are able to make a strong point without attacking your prospect's position or ego. Basically you are telling your prospect that he would have to be a real putz if he didn't learn from this other fellow's misfortune. In many cases, this helps bring your prospect around without causing any fireworks.

Be street smart, have third party stories available in your selling skills bag so you can make a point without getting into an argument with one of your prospects. It will lead to many diplomatic sales.

❑ WHEN TO HANDLE AN OBJECTION

Street smart salesmen know that the best time to answer a prospect's objection is immediately. The worst thing you can do is try to slide over or avoid answering his objection altogether.

By responding quickly to a prospect's objection, you are telling him that you care about him, you are listening to what he has to say. This builds trust and rapport between you and your prospect, which will go a long way towards making the sale.

If you do not immediately answer what is on your prospect's mind, the only thing that he will be thinking about during your sales presentation is why the heck you didn't answer his question. A prospect who is not concentrating on you, as well as on your product or service, will be one impossible prospect to sell.

After answering his question, and before you move on with your presentation, make sure his objection is answered to his satisfaction. Get an agreement before continuing.

Salesman: George, do you now see how you will benefit from this?

Customer: Now I do.

Be street smart—don't put off for later what you can answer right now; for if you do delay, it just might cost you later.

Tactics for Handling Objections

Handling objections properly is critical if you are to become a street smart salesman, earning those large commission checks. This is the area where we separate the achievers from the nonachievers. If you are able to answer your prospect's objections to his satisfaction, you should then be able to move smoothly into the final stage of your sales call, which is closing the sale.

Underachievers handle customer objections as if they were trying to do ballet in work boots. They are awkward and clumsy.

Handling objections does not mean that you try to outsmart your prospect by some slick flim-flam response to his question or objection. That is not the case. Handling objections means that you are able to gain the confidence of your prospect by answering his concerns in a logical and convincing manner. The tactics that I have provided for you in this section are based on years of experience in handling prospects' objections successfully. Read, study, and practice these tactics; before long you will be doing perfect pirouettes!

❑ THE TACTIC OF QUESTIONING AND LISTENING

The street smart salesman is keenly aware that there isn't a better technique for uncovering and answering customer objections than the questioning process. The street smart salesman knows that when he is at the top of his game, closing a high percentage of sales, it is because he is asking the right questions and listening ever so carefully to his customer's responses. Only through this process of asking questions and listening to his prospect's answers can the street smart salesman truly determine what is important to his customers. And that's the key: questions help to get your prospect talking in such a manner that either he ends up selling himself or gives you enough information whereby you have the ammunition to overcome any of his concerns.

There are five different kinds of questions that a street smart salesman uses in order to overcome customer objections. Read, study, and practice using these questioning tactics. You will be pleasantly surprised how much easier it will be for you to handle your prospects' objections in the future.

"Why" Questions

Street smart salesmen use "why" questions in order to get a better understanding as to why their prospects feel a certain way. The following examples will illustrate my point:

Prospect: I'm not interested.

Salesman: Why do you feel that way?

By using "why" questions and sounding sincere and concerned, there is an excellent chance that you will discover the real reason as to what is holding back your prospect from purchasing. Once you have learned what is holding your prospect back, you will be in a position to handle his concerns. Until then you will be dealing with irrelevant excuses.

Information Questions

Street smart salesmen use questions in order to get new information. Often, this will help to inform you if circumstances that would either help or hurt your chances of making a sale have changed:

- "George, are you still having delivery problems?"

- "Bob, are you still using the same supplier for all your widgets?"

- "Is Mr. Brown still in charge of purchasing?"

Use these types of questions. You can never have too much information. Give your prospects a chance of telling you how things are, it's the street smart thing to do.

Additional Questions

This type of question helps the street smart salesman get additional information by allowing his prospect to discuss any other concerns that he has not voiced.

George, are there any other concerns or reasons that you have in mind, in addition to the one you already mentioned, for not wanting to purchase?

In many instances, prospects will not resent questions phrased this way. Quite often you will discover that your prospect will then give you additional concerns that he has for refusing to buy. At this point you will have a clear picture as to what you are up against.

Open-Ended Questions

Open-ended questions are used by the street smart salesman in order to encourage his prospect to speak freely about a topic of his interest. It stimulates the customer to give added information on something already stated.

Salesman: You said before that you have had some problems. Could you tell me about them?

Prospect: Well, for the past three years we have been losing about 10 percent of our customer base because of poor quality control. Not only that, but our costs keep going up, etc.

These kinds of questions are especially effective when you are trying to gather information from a client who may have trouble expressing himself. Open-ended questions require thought on your prospect's part.

Closed-Ended Questions

The street smart salesman uses closed-ended questions in order to steer the conversation to a specific topic of his choosing and limit his customer's responses mostly to short answers.

Salesman: Are you having problems increasing your customer base?

Prospect: Yes I am.

This type of question is also helpful to the street smart salesman when he is confronted with a customer who has a tendency to go off on tangents. It helps the street smart salesman regain control of the sales call, bringing his prospect's attention back to the subject at hand.

You will find that this questioning tactic can be used for any given situation. The more you practice using questions, the more comfortable and effective you will become. If a client says, "I'm not interested," from now on you will ask, "What seems to concern you?" If a client says, "This is more then I am willing to spend," you will ask, "How much do you want to spend?" If your client says, "You're the best salesman I have ever met," ask him, "What do you like about me?"

By listening carefully to his client's responses, the street smart salesman gathers valuable information that makes it easier for him to handle customer objections. Often a prospect will give you so much information, you will be able to overcome his objections by saying, "Based on what you've said. . . ," which is just about the most effective way of getting a client to commit to purchase. After all, if a prospect makes a statement, it is a fact; if you as a salesman make the same statement, it is considered a sales pitch.

In addition to giving you valuable information, responding to a prospect with a question will also provide you with valuable time in which you can collect your thoughts. During this time, you can map out an intelligent strategy to successfully answer whatever objection that your prospect brings up. Begin to use phrases such as:

- "What do you think?"
- "Why do you ask?"
- "What is your opinion?"
- "How does it appear to you?"

The street smart salesman uses this questioning technique so often that when someone happens to ask him how he feels, he responds, "How should I feel?"

Use this questioning tool; it will effectively help you to answer whatever objections that your prospect might come up with. More importantly, by using a few well-placed questions, you are always in control of your presentation, leading it in whatever direction that you want it to take.

Be street smart, question everything; it will provide you with all the right sales answers!

❏ PRODUCT COMPARISON

As I stated earlier in the chapter dealing with constructing a presentation, it is extremely important for you to know the strengths and weaknesses of your products as well as your competitor's products.

If you find that one of your prospects is basing his decision to purchase your product on a comparison with a competitor's product, it is essential that you be aware of all the advantages and disadvantages of each. If a prospect indicates that your products or services are more expensive than your competitor's, only if you have a clear understanding of why they are more expensive will you be able to turn a negative concern into a positive benefit for your client to purchase. The increased cost may be attributed to a higher quality of material that goes into the manufacturing of your product, which in the long term will prove to be the better purchase for your client. Your product knowledge, of yours as well as your competitor's product, should be so strong that you are able to point out all the unique strengths of your products or services that could make the difference between making the sale or not.

❏ GUARANTEES

A primary concern of many individuals when they are about to make the decision to purchase is that they are getting taken. One of the best sales tools that you have for relieving this kind of anxiety and concern is your company's or manufacturer's guarantee. If your product or service comes with a guarantee, use it to overcome your prospect's objection to purchase. A guarantee tells your prospect that he is getting exactly what you have promised he would get, without having to take your word for it.

Often, by going over your contract and indicating how it gives buyer protection, you will find that much of your prospect's resistance to buy will disappear.

❏ THIRD PARTY STORIES

A salesman who does not have a whole bunch of third party stories is severely limiting his chances of making sales.

As I wrote earlier in the chapter, third party stories are an excellent way of making a point by describing another individual who was in a similar situation. Depending upon the point that you wish to make, you can manipulate your story in whatever direction will hit home the hardest with your customer, without getting into a confrontation with him.

Third party stories also help you to create positive emotional responses from your prospect such as the feeling of opportunity, excitement, etc.

You as a salesman can utilize third party stories to indicate to your prospect that you are a caring and honest person.

❑ "BUT" TACTIC

This is a simple tactic that can be used to give your prospect a bit more information without getting into a confrontation with him.

- "George, I can appreciate what you are saying, *but* if you would consider this new bit of information it just might make you change your mind."

- "George, I understand the point that you are trying to make, *but* I don't believe you are taking these points into consideration."

Be street smart, use this tactic; it can help you get another shot at a prospect who can be an obstinate pain in the butt!

As you now have learned, answering objections does not mean that you have to use a lot of slick, fast talking in order to convince your prospect that he should buy from you.

Be street smart—ask the right questions in order to get the right answers, which will enable you to successfully overcome many of your prospect's objections to purchase. And by the way, the next time someone asks you how you feel, ask them, "How should I feel?"

The following questions are designed to get you to think like a street smart salesman with respect to answering customer objections. Read these questions carefully and answer them either in your mind or on a sheet of paper.

1. Do you consider your prospect's objections your best friend on a sales call?

2. If not, why not?

3. What are the most frequent objections that you come across?

4. Which objection do you have the most difficulty overcoming?

5. Why?

6. Do you use the questioning technique in trying to overcome customer objections?

7. If not, why not?

8. Specifically, how would you use the following types of questions when encountering customer objections:
   a) Why questions
   b) Information questions
   c) Additional questions
   d) Open-ended questions
   e) Closed-ended questions

Now that you have completed this chapter, you should have a much better understanding as to how to answer your prospect's objections. If you still feel that your prospect's objections are your own worst enemy, then I suggest that either you reread this chapter carefully and practice the skills to handle objections or think about another profession that will not give you as much anxiety. However, if you feel that your new best friend happens to be your prospect's objections, then you have taken a quantum leap towards becoming a street smart salesman!

12
Closing

A close is a specific tactic used by the street smart salesman to influence a prospect into making a positive decision in his favor. Closing is the culmination of all the preparation and work that the street smart salesman has put in. Only when he gets a prospect to say, "Yes, I will do business with you," is it considered a closed sale, and that is the bottom line for these apt salesmen; everything else is meaningless.

Street smart salesmen know only too well that companies do not pay commission to salespeople who try hard and almost make the sale. "Almost" sales do not pay the mortgage, "almost" sales do not buy *you* all the wonderful adult toys that are available. Only signed contracts from customers who want to use your products or services have any worth.

Knowing that the only way that they can earn big bucks is to bring in signed contracts, street smart salesmen are relentless in their pursuit to close the deal. The very first moment that a street smart salesman meets his prospect, he has only one thought in mind, to concentrate his efforts to get the job done, to close that sale!

There is nothing more challenging to the street smart salesman than having the ability to influence a prospect to make a positive decision in his favor; and when he does, this skillful achiever experiences an exhilarating high that motivates him to persevere until he is able to close the next deal.

The closing tactics of the fakers, takers and makers are so limited that it becomes virtually impossible for these under-achievers to successfully close their sales on a consistent basis. Their closing attempts are often awkward, clumsy, inappropri-ate and amateurish, which makes it quite easy for their pros-pects to reject their offerings. At times, these underachievers are so ill at ease in a closing situation that they even become hesitant to ask for the order.

Underachievers are not professional closers; they do not con-sistently get the job done. When they close a sale, more often than not it is out of chance rather than as a result of their sales skills. Prospects buy products or services from these fakers, takers, and makers more often than not because they are needed badly, not because they were sold by a salesman who skillfully disclosed a client need or want that would best be satisfied by his product or service.

If you are a salesman who suffers from sweaty palms associ-ated with closing, causing you to be uncomfortable as well as hesitant to ask for the order, it is time that you develop strong, sound, money-making street smart closing tactics.

This chapter will provide you with loads of ammunition for becoming a professional street smart closer. These tactics are the ones being utilized daily by those who have achieved enor-mous success by consistently closing their sales. Become street smart; read carefully and get the job done!

The Street Smart Chameleon

Street smart salesmen are not lucky when they sell to a cus-tomer; nobody can be consistently lucky. They have a high closing rate because they have in their bag of selling skills a number of effective closing techniques that enable them to persuasively convince their prospects to purchase. These clever salesmen have many options when they close, never having to be dependent on one or two tactics; if they were, they certainly would not be able to handle all the various customer personalities and sales situations that they encounter on a daily basis in the real world of selling. Street smart salesmen understand that there is no one magical close that works everytime. Even if they have had success with a particular closing tactic nine straight times, they are aware that it just might not cut it the tenth time, and street smart salesmen always prepare themselves for that tenth time, the unexpected situation!

Throughout this chapter, we will discuss in detail the different kinds of closes that you can use in your day-to-day selling. Street smart salesmen are successful because they have the ability to recognize which specific closing technique to use in order to motivate and convince their prospects to buy.

Street smart salesmen also have the ability to adapt to the personalities of their prospects, which helps these adroit chameleon-like salesmen build trust and rapport between themselves and their clients. This is essential if you are to become a consistent closer.

Underachievers do not adapt their selling techniques to anyone; they treat all their customers as if they had the same personality. It is no wonder that they do not close consistently, losing many opportunities to earn those large commission checks. Instead of realizing that they are not connecting on a personal level with their clients, they blame their lack of success on their prospects, accusing them of just shopping around, of not really being interested in buying.

Street smart salesmen know that if they don't connect with their prospects, they have no one to blame but themselves, and they work hard to connect. They want those big bucks, and like chameleons, these savvy salesmen are able to adapt to their prospects' personalities. Street smart salesmen can be comical, serious, creative, straightforward, haughty, or down and dirty. Whatever it takes, these achievers have the strategy to relate to their clients.

❏ SERIOUS STREET SMART CHAMELEON TACTICS

If a street smart salesman finds himself selling a prospect who is serious and not interested in small talk, he makes sure that he does not go off on a tangent; he sticks close to his presentation and answers all his customer's questions in a clear and forthright manner.

A tactic used by the street smart salesman when faced with this solemn type of client is to slow down his speech, pausing every so often, projecting a feeling that he as a salesman is giving serious thought to his prospect's needs and concerns. In addition, he keeps his posture erect, never slouching, which would convey a more relaxed, informal, and less serious mood.

By using these tactics you will discover that prospects with sober personalities will relate to you; but more importantly, they buy from people whom they relate to, which is the bottom line!

❏ OUTGOING STREET SMART CHAMELEON TACTICS

On the other hand, if a street smart salesman finds himself in front of a prospect who is open, friendly, or quick to laugh, our artful chameleon becomes Bob Hope, which greatly enhances his chances of successfully closing the sale.

A less formal presentation is the tactic used by the street smart salesman in selling to a client with this type of personality. Small talk can be used, while you attentively listen and observe what might be of interest to your customer, such as discussing sports, your client's children, or a particular piece of jewelry that he may be wearing. On these occasions it is a good idea to have one or two good jokes tucked away.

Your posture is not formal; crossing your legs, as well as supporting your smiling face in your hands, is perfectly okay. Statements like, "You are one fun guy," "You must have been some wild kid growing up," said in a laughing tone, sometimes will help you to connect with these types of clients.

Remember, don't get so relaxed that you are not concentrating on the reason that you are there, to close the deal; that's the bottom line, no kidding!

Now that you understand the importance of adapting to the personality of your client, use these street smart tactics to make a connection. If you find it is not in your personality to adapt to different types of people, closing consistently will be a problem for you. But, if you can become a chameleon, you have taken a giant step towards becoming a successful street smart closer!

Trial Close

A trial close is used by the street smart salesman in order to get an indication as to how positive or negative his prospect may be at a certain point in his presentation; it allows you to test the waters. The advantage of using trial closes is that they afford you the flexibility of asking for the order without risking a halt to your presentation.

In most cases, a prospect will not cut you off completely by giving you a simple "no" when he indicates that he is not going to buy; on many occasions, he will tell you the definite reason why he is hesitant to commit to purchase. This gives the street smart salesman an opportunity to concentrate on his client's area of concern, directing his presentation where the emphasis is most needed.

On the other hand, you may try a trial close and your prospect may give you full indication that he is absolutely ready to buy, in which case you should forget the rest of your presentation and go right for the close. Listed below are some examples of how a street smart salesman phrases a trial close:

1. George, are you buying for investment or pleasure?

2. Would you want the red widgets or the blue ones?

3. When we start working with you, you'll quickly see the difference in service.

4. I hope I can squeeze you in as soon as next week.

Remember, if you get a "no" it is not the end of your presentation. Many times a street smart salesman will trial close early in the sales call, often getting a "no." He simply replies, "George, I get so excited talking about my product, sometimes I forget to give you all the pertinent information so you can make a positive decision, and that's just what I did with you. Of course you can't make a positive decision based on what I've told you." This allows our street smart salesman to continue his sales call. Notice how clever he was when he told his client that once he had all the pertinent information he would be able to make a positive decision.

All salesmen should practice using trial closes; they help to condition your prospects into saying "yes." If you wait until the very end of your presentations to try to get a commitment, you are putting too much pressure on the decision-making capabilities of your clients.

Emotional Appeal Selling

Street smart salesmen realize that in many instances individuals purchase what they want based on emotion, not necessarily what they need based on logic. When people choose to buy expensive pieces of jewelry, they do so not because they need the jewelry in order to survive, but because, emotionally, buying it makes them feel good. Street smart salesmen work hard to discover just what an individual's emotional needs are, and as soon as they determine them, they work extremely hard to satisfy these needs. This allows the street smart salesmen to close many a profitable deal.

The following examples will indicate to you just how many different types of emotional closes there are; after all, as individuals we are emotional animals, motivated by many different factors. These various closes will give you an idea how emotional selling can be a useful tactic for closing a sale.

❏ THE EGO CLOSE

I know a very successful exotic–car saleswoman. On many occasions she has told me that if her customers bought strictly on logic she would never have made a sale. After all, how practical is it to drive a car that cost $100,000 to the local mall?

Knowing the reasons why her customers buy is an enormous help to her when she goes for the close.

The initial tactic that she uses when a prospect shows interest in a particular automobile is to get him behind the wheel for a test drive. Understanding that image is important to her clients, she issues sporadic, but well-planned statements such as: "Mr./Mrs./Ms. _____, you look fantastic behind that wheel, that car is really you"; "I don't know what kind of business you're in, but obviously you have to be successful to be considering a motor car of this magnitude. Doesn't it make you feel as if you are out in front of a parade?"; "Not too many people are fortunate enough to own a motor car such as this, you must be real proud of yourself." (Notice how she uses the word motor car, never saying car; this adds a snob appeal to her product.)

By the time her clients have finished road testing that particular automobile, they feel an emotional need to own it. Logic doesn't come into play, allowing our street smart saleswoman to earn many large commission checks.

This street smart auto saleswoman was able to create an image of what owning that car would mean to her prospect on an emotional level, allowing his heart instead of his head to make the decision to purchase.

❏ "DON'T YOU CARE?" CLOSE

The street smart salesman creates an emotional image in the mind of his prospect that if he doesn't take action to purchase, he will be negatively affecting his loved ones. This tactic is based on the fact that most people find it a lot easier to say no if they believe it might only affect themselves; they do not feel real comfortable gambling with their loved ones' lives.

George, it is true that this safety feature will further add
to your costs; but if your loved ones are ever in an
accident, it will most likely save their lives. Isn't it worth
the added cost?

Can you imagine what it would take for this prospect to say
the safety of his family just isn't worth the added cost, especially if his wife and kids are present? For that prospect to say
no, either he would have to be one heartless S.O.B. or planning
on taking the first plane out of the country.

This tactic can be used when selling any kind of safety
products for the home, car, workplace, etc.

❏ THE INTANGIBLE FANTASY CLOSE

In the intangible fantasy close, street smart salesmen are able to
paint picture images of what a prospect would hope to have
one day; and they know how to paint, they are the Picassos of
word images. By the time the street smart salesman is finished
creating his word images, his prospects can vividly picture
their dreams right before their eyes. This tactic is especially
effective because fantasies are a lot more majestic, fun, and less
costly than the reality of it.

Mrs. _____, can you see how beautiful your home will
look over there on that knoll? Are you going to have
large windows so you can take advantage of that magnificent panoramic view?—it sure looks like God's country.

This street smart salesman created an image of a home that
not only is not there, but may never be built. He created hope
and dreams for his prospect. His use of the phrase "God's
country" conjured up all sorts of positive emotional feelings on
the part of his customer. Anybody selling an intangible item
can create images that might be far greater than the ones that
will become reality, and this will lead to sales.

❑ "REST ASSURED" CLOSE

By using this tactic, the street smart salesman is able to create an emotional image in the mind of his prospect that he no longer will have to twist and turn at night worrying about a particular aspect of his life. In the pressured world that we live in today, individuals appreciate and are willing to pay in order to "rest assured" about a particular concern.

> This insurance policy will insure that your children will be provided for in case of your death. Isn't it worth the added premium for the peace of mind knowing that their educational needs are going to be taken care of?

The street smart salesman is creating a feeling in his prospect's mind that if anything happens to him, he can rest assured that his children will be taken care of. This tactic can be used by anyone who is offering a product or service that will give a feeling of peace of mind. Here's how an attorney would use this tactic.

> If you do not spend the money now to update your contracts, insuring that they are foolproof and will protect you as well as your company, you may wake up one day without the company that you worked so hard to build. Isn't it worth the added cost to rest assured that this will never happen?

In summary, street smart salesmen are able to size up their prospects on an emotional level. They never assume what motivates them to buy. These proficient salesmen are aware that there will be times when a customer will initially talk about price, price, price; but after further investigation, the street smart salesman will discover that the customer has emotional wants and needs, which often take precedence over price. Street smart salesmen also understand that the more they can create emotional satisfaction for their prospects, the higher the price their customers will be willing to pay and the easier the close. Be street smart—don't always sell to the head; after all, the heart is where the "rest assured" sale lies!

Quality Selling

Quality selling is based on the fact that your products or services are really good and, in many instances, are superior to your competition's.

Street smart salesmen like to sell the quality of their product or service. They know that then their prospects will not be as price conscious and will be willing to overlook higher cost or later deliveries.

The quality, puppy dog, inventory, and Ben Franklin closes are utilized by street smart salesmen in order to get their prospects to purchase based on the quality of their products or services.

❏ QUALITY CLOSE

The quality close is based on the premise that people are really interested in quality when they make a purchase. Individuals may want to buy cheap, but street smart salesmen know they do not want to buy garbage.

Salesman: George, I cannot lower my price any further, and the reason for that is based entirely on the fact that my company made a commitment to clients like yourself.

Customer: What do you mean?

Salesman: My company many years ago made the decision that it would be much easier to explain price one time only, rather than apologizing for poor quality forever. Knowing this, George, I am sure you are glad we made that pledge.

What is this prospect going to say, "No, I like buying junk"? The street smart salesman knows for the most part that his prospects are not going to respond by saying that quality is not important. If you have a quality product or service, tell your prospects about it; it will close sales for you.

❏ PUPPY DOG CLOSE

The puppy dog close is utilized by all street smart salesmen who are selling a quality product that can be left behind with a prospect to use for an agreed time and, if not totally satisfied, not be obligated to purchase.

The theory behind this close, like the parents who take a puppy dog home for their children and quickly fall in love with the dog, is that the customer will never consider giving the product back.

This can only be done with a superior product that will indeed make prospects want to own it after using it. Obviously, if they have any sort of difficulty with your product or service, they will gladly want you to take it back.

> George, why don't I just leave my copying machine here for two weeks. I'm willing to do this because I know our system is superior to anything you have seen or used. Be my guest; if you don't want it after the two weeks, there is no obligation on your part; I will gladly take it back.

Any salesman selling a quality product that can be left behind or a service that can be used on a trial basis can use the puppy dog close, relying on the fact that once his prospects get used to their new conveniences they will never want to give them back!

❏ BEN FRANKLIN CLOSE

This close is based on the fact that whenever Ben Franklin had an important decision to make, he would take out a piece of paper and divide it into two columns. At the top of one side of the paper he would write "pros," and on the top of the other side of paper he would write "cons." He then would list all the positive reasons and all the negative reasons for making a decision, and when he finished with this exercise, Franklin would see which side outweighed the other.

The street smart salesman, knowing that the quality of his product will deliver far more benefits than drawbacks, will use this very same exercise in getting his customer to make a decision to purchase. The street smart salesman first describes how Franklin utilized this two-column process to assure himself that he indeed would make the best decision possible. Then the street smart salesman has his prospect write down the pros and cons of purchasing his product.

Pros	*Cons*
1. More dependable	1. Price slightly higher.
2. Easier to maintain	
3. Will increase production	
4. Always in stock.	

As you can see for yourself George, the pros certainly outweigh the cons. Look at the benefits that you will derive just by paying slightly more than you are used to. You can see in black and white that the quality will make it less expensive in the long run.

This tactic also gives you an opportunity to hear what concerns your customers have, which you then can try to overcome at a later point in the sales call if they are still holding up your prospect from moving forward.

❏ INVENTORY CLOSE

This tactic is used when a prospect indicates that he could get a faster delivery date if he ordered from a competitor. The street smart salesman's answer is a logical and effective close.

Salesman: George, what does it tell you about my product that I can't keep enough in stock.

Prospect: It tells me that you don't make enough.

Salesman: No, George, it tells you because of our superior quality there is a huge demand for our product, that it's a product worth waiting for, and that's why you want it.

The puppy dog, quality, Ben Franklin, and inventory closes give the street smart salesman an opportunity to make sales based on quality, with less emphasis on price. Street smart salesmen do not want to rely on being the cheapest guys in town; companies do not pay large commissions for that kind of sales approach. Be street smart—sell the quality of your product; it's worth it!

Benefit Selling

Benefit selling is used to indicate to a prospect that the quicker he makes a decision to purchase, the greater the reward to him. Street smart salesmen use this close effectively in order to create urgency on the part of their customers to buy. Urgency, the fear of losing out on an opportunity, is a heck of a motivator; and if the sense of urgency is used effectively, customers will buy.

❑ THREE QUESTION BENEFIT CLOSE

The street smart salesman asks his clients three questions that lead them to the conclusion that the longer they wait to purchase, the more it will cost them. The street smart salesman words his questions in such a manner that his prospects would appear to be foolish if they did not agree to purchase:

1. "George, can you see where this would save you money?"

2. "Are you interested in saving money?"

3. "If you were to become interested in starting to save money, when do you think would be the best time to start?"

Here is another example:

1. "Tom, can you see how this machine will make your factory more efficient?"

2. "Are you interested in running a more efficient factory?"

3. "When do you think it would be the best time to begin running your factory more efficiently?"

Observe how the street smart salesman controls where he wants to go in the close. The answers are obvious; and if he should get a negative response, he has a strong, logical chance to overcome any objections that his client may come up with.

❑ BENEFIT BY OTHERS' MISFORTUNE CLOSE

This close is based on the fact that individuals love to get bargains, and they especially feel that they made a good deal when they are able to profit from someone else's misfortunes. Aware of this, the street smart salesman uses this close in the following way:

- "Mr./Mrs./Ms. Brown, I can give it to you at this price because the other couple just could not keep up their payments. As a result, you will be able to take advantage of what they already put into the deal."

- "This house is worth much more money, but since the owners are going through a difficult divorce, they are willing to let it go for that price. If you move quickly, you can take advantage of this situation."

- "You are really lucky, the only reason this is available is due to the fact that the other people could not get the credit; if you move quickly, you can take advantage of the situation."

This is a fantastic close; when using it you will see how individuals will move quickly once they see how they can benefit from another person's misfortune.

"Give Them What They Want" Selling

"Give them what they want" selling is based on the fact that you have gone through your entire presentation, wherein your prospect has given all indication that your product or service meets his needs and wants and that he is ready to purchase.

Once the prospect has made the commitment to buy, the street smart salesman asks for the order in a matter-of-fact manner by using the assumptive and alternate of choice closes. This is important, for if you sound nervous, surprised, or excited when you assume the sale is made, it might scare your prospect into thinking that he has indeed made too fast a decision.

❑ ASSUMPTIVE CLOSE

The assumptive close is used by the street smart salesman when he has gone through his entire presentation, all along getting positive answers to his trial closes. The street smart salesman assumes then that it is a natural process for his client to buy and makes a closing statement such as, "George, all you have to do is sign here and I will get you immediate delivery," or "Please hand me the phone so I can call in your order."

If your prospect does not object, then your deal is closed, without your actually having to ask for a decision on his part.

❏ ALTERNATE OF CHOICE CLOSE

An alternate of choice close is based on a salesman's asking a question that leaves no room for his prospect to indicate anything but that a sale has been made. As in the assumptive close, the street smart salesman uses this tactic if his prospect has indicated all along that he has no objections to purchasing.

- "George, do you want one or two dozen?"

- "Which do you prefer, delivery on Wednesday or Thursday?"

- "Do you want the deluxe model or the super deluxe?"

- "Which do you prefer, ordering the green ones or the blue ones?"

If the client should happen to answer that he is not interested in either choice, the street smart salesman, as in all closes that may not work, then goes through the process discussed in the chapter on handling objections, trying to isolate what his prospect's concerns are. Knowing this is more than half the battle in making a sale.

Price Selling

Street smart salesmen are aware that it is impossible to always get top price for their products or services. The difference between the underachiever and the street smart salesman is the fact that the underachiever starts out low in price to begin with and goes lower to close his deals, whereas the street smart salesman starts out at a higher price and, only through negotiations and commitments made by his prospect, chooses to bend his price. He does not discount his price easily as if it were coming to his customer all along.

The street smart salesman uses the following tactics when he realizes that he has to negotiate price in order to close a deal. By using these tactics, even though he might have to lower his price, he often is able to obtain an added benefit for himself or his company that will make the deal more palatable. Study and use these tactics; they apply to many different selling situations.

❏ MORE FOR LESS PRICE CLOSE

If a street smart salesman is representing a product that can be purchased in quantities, he offers a lower price based on his prospect's ability to buy in larger amounts.

> George, we can agree on this price, all you have to do is buy an extra gross. You drive a hard bargain, but I'll do it.

Notice how the street smart salesman assumes that his customer will take the extra amount. This is a form of an assumptive close, which we discussed earlier in this chapter.

❏ ADD ON PRICE CLOSE

Cash discounts can be offered to customers based on their purchasing additional items that you sell.

> Miss, I can only sell you this camera for that price as long as you agree to purchase an additional ten rolls of film.

❏ CASH AND CARRY PRICE CLOSE

Street smart salesmen can offer discounts to customers who agree to pay on better terms, such as cash on delivery (C.O.D.).

> George, it is extremely difficult for me to give you that kind of price. The only way that I can possibly see my way clear to do it is if you agree to pay C.O.D.

❏ REFERRAL PRICE CLOSE

Street smart salesmen will lower their price if their customers will recommend other potential clients to them.

> George, I will lower my price on the condition that you will agree to try to refer other customers to me. I know if you agree to this, it will not be an idle promise on your part just to get a special price.

Notice how the street smart salesman used the words "on the condition that you will agree to this," instead of "the condition that you say you will," which does not carry as strong a commitment. In addition, he reinforces this commitment by indicating that he only agreed to lower his price because he believes his client is a man of his word. This now makes his client feel emotionally obligated not to go back on his word.

❏ IMMEDIACY PRICE CLOSE

Street smart salesmen will give discounts to clients who agree to take immediate delivery.

> Tom, I can only give you that kind of deal if you agree to take immediate delivery. If I have to hold it in my warehouse one extra day, I just cannot do it.

❏ REDUCE TO THE SMALLEST VARIABLE PRICE CLOSE

The street smart salesman shrewdly uses this tactic to overcome price objections by breaking down the difference between what his prospect wants to pay and what he wants to sell for into its smallest component. By doing so, the street smart salesman can get his prospect to understand that what he is arguing so strongly about just isn't that important.

- George, I know this house has to be sold for $63,000 and that you wanted to spend only $53,000, but based on what you've said, this house is everything you wanted it to be, and you can fully expect to live in it for the next twenty years. The $10,000 difference is what we are talking about; and divided over twenty years, it comes out to less than $10 a week. Is that what is going to keep you from purchasing your dream house?"

- "Mr. and Mrs. Smith, I know our oil is 5¢ higher than you are presently paying, but based on what you've said, you would feel more secure for your family by using a full service oil company, never having to worry about keeping your family warm in the winter. You told me you burn a thousand gallons of oil per year, which comes out to about $1.00 a week more than you are currently paying. Knowing all this now, doesn't it make sense to have all this security for only a dollar?"

In many instances, the street smart salesman who uses this tactic is able to get his prospect to realize that to deny himself the benefits of the product is ridiculous.

The key to negotiating price is to make sure that if you have to lower your price, you lower it in such a fashion that your prospect believes he is fortunate to get it. The tactic used by the street smart salesman is to give in slowly when he negotiates. He also knows to concede in small increments; why give away the store if you don't have to? The street smart salesman tries to close by splitting the difference as opposed to dropping his price all the way down. But most importantly, if you agree to lower your price, make sure it is based on the fact that your prospect has committed himself to buy. After giving away the store, many underachievers find out that they still have not made the sale. Be street smart—if you are going to give, make sure you are also going to receive!

Concession Selling

Concession selling is when you have to give up something in order to make a deal. It personally grieves me to give anything away; however, in the real world, street smart salesmen know that we have to do what we have to do. The old saying, "Half a pie is better than no pie at all," relates to this kind of selling, although the street smart salesman works really hard not to give away a single piece too easily.

❏ CONTINGENCY CONCESSION CLOSE

The street smart salesman restates his offer to his customers so that the decision to purchase is dependent upon some other factors that normally would not be offered.

- "George, if I could get the company to go along with giving you a loaner car, then would you order the car today?"

- "If I can get you an exclusive distributorship for the line, will you take it in by the end of the month?"

❏ GIVE AWAY CONCESSION CLOSE

This close happens when the street smart salesman offers an added incentive to his prospect if he agrees to buy that very moment. This is only offered as the last resort and at the very end of the sales call. The street smart salesman doesn't want his prospects to think that they can get even more products or services for free.

- "George, if you can take six today, I can throw in two extra."
- "If you take delivery of the car today, I can give you free rust proofing."

The important thing to remember when you have to make concessions, is to be sure that the deal can actually be made. You don't want to work really hard, losing valuable selling time, only to agree to something that just can't be done. Know what you can give, and give in a fashion whereby your prospect feels he has made the best deal possible.

Nothing to Lose Selling

This kind of selling is tried only after you have totally exhausted all other tactics. The nothing to lose selling can be a lot of fun, simply because you can do whatever, because you have nothing to lose! In some instances by being funny, outrageous, or different, you will be surprised by a prospect who will change around his negative thinking.

Remember, after you've spent a lot of time with your prospect and are about to leave, you can give it one more college try by using these tactics. Be street smart—have some fun with it; it just might surprise you.

❏ NEGATIVE CLOSE

This close is based on the fact that people want things they cannot have. If all else is not working, sometimes a client can be sold when he believes he is going to lose out on an opportunity. When you see you are going nowhere in closing and, in fact, start to feel that you are turning off your client altogether, begin to pack up your materials and say the following:

> George, I do not want you to feel like I am shoving my product down your throat. I should never have to do that, representing this kind of quality product. As a representative of this company for many years, I know that not all people can see the advantages of my product, and as a result, it is not for everybody, and obviously it is not for you.

After making this statement, continue ever so slowly to pack up, and make sure you keep your mouth closed. Often you will hear your customer say, "I didn't say it wasn't for me," whereupon you respond, "Then let's get the deal done." The prospect, seeing that you are taking the opportunity to buy away from him, will often come around and decide to purchase.

❏ COLOMBO CLOSE

This close is based on Peter Falk's detective character, Lieutenant Colombo. Invariably, as he is about to leave his suspect, giving the criminal false security, he turns and asks, "Do you mind if I ask you a question?" whereby he opens up a full discussion with hopes of getting valuable information.

The street smart salesman does the same thing. He pretends to be finished with his sales call, actually packing up his materials, which relaxes his prospect and makes him think that the presentation is over; and before he gets up to leave, our savvy salesman asks:

Salesman: Do you mind if I ask you one question, George?

Customer: Sure, fire away.

Salesman: Is it the fact that you did not have faith in me and my company that held you up from ordering?

Customer:	No, you seem to be an ethical guy.
Salesman:	Was it the fact that you thought our price was too high?
Customer:	No, your price seemed reasonable.

The street smart salesman will go on and on, covering all the significant points in his presentation, until he comes across the objection that was not answered satisfactorily, giving him another opportunity to try to overcome it.

On the other hand, if the street smart salesman goes through all his questions and does not get a negative answer, he simply turns toward his prospect and says, "George, if you are so satisfied with everything, why not move forward to secure the goods needed?" At that point, keep your mouth shut and wait for your customer's answer. In many instances the client will give you a "yes" to move forward; but if you should happen to get a "no," you still have a chance to try to discover what his real reason is for holding back from buying. The last tactic used at this point is simply to say, "George, I'm leaving; I do not want to pressure you to say 'yes'; that's not my style (make sure you keep a straight and sincere face when you utter these white lies); but for my own edification, why the heck aren't you saying 'yes'? Based upon what you've said, I know you are pleased with the benefits of my product." Again keep quiet; at this point your client may be worn down and will give you the real reason why he does not want to buy, which is all you can hope for.

❏ DEMAND THE ORDER CLOSE

I do not suggest that you use this close with an ex-football player, but if you read your client as a person who might purchase if you assert yourself, give it a shot.

George, I've been coming to see you for three years, and I'm tired of leaving without an order. I don't care how

long I have to sit here, I'm not leaving without an order.
Once you give me the opportunity to work with you, I
know you're going to love to do business with us.

Look right into his eyes when you say that, indicating that
you mean business. Sometimes a prospect will throw you a
bone just to get rid of you; but by chance if you happen to have
misread him and your prospect starts to charge at you with
malice in his eyes, it's best to leave. Seriously, some prospects
like salesmen who are assertive; it shows them you have confidence in yourself as well as your product.

❏ THE POOR SOUL CLOSE

This close is based on the fact that people, and prospects are
people, have a heart and are apt to give someone down on his
luck a break. Remember, don't be depressed by using this
close, it is only a tactic, and you are using it because you have
nothing to lose!

Mr. Brown, I need this sale real bad. If I don't bring in
some business, it might be my job, and I have three
kids.

Not a bad touch by throwing in the line about the kids; after
all, nobody wants to see kids starve.

❏ "POLEASE" CLOSE

This close can be pretty funny if you have a sense of humor.
Simply put, it is based on the theory of begging, and some
street smart salesmen are good beggars. When using this close,
think of Bambi when he learns that his mom is dead; it helps to
create pathos between you and your prospect.

Polease (What he is saying is please, but if you whine and beg properly, it comes out *polease*) Mr. Brown, give me the order, polease.

Now, you may feel this kind of approach can be degrading or humilitating, and I guess to the average salesman it is. But not to the street smart salesman. He is a fox; he will do whatever it takes to make the sale. Remember, he who laughs last often cashes the largest commission checks. Be street smart—be polite and *polease* ask for the order!

☐ THE CARD COMMITMENT CLOSE

The card commitment close is used by the street smart salesman in order to get a commitment for a future appointment to discuss whatever proposal has been made. The street smart salesman is aware that he will lose an opportunity to close a sale if he merely hands a prospect his business card without trying to obtain some kind of commitment.

Often, when a prospect asks for your card at the end of your presentation without giving you a positive decision to purchase, he does so more as a polite formality than anything else. Instead of handing his card over and walking away with nothing more than hope, a street smart salesman would handle it in this fashion:

Salesman: "George, you obviously want my business card so that we can get together to discuss my proposal at greater lengths, isn't that so?"

Prospect: "Absolutely."

Salesman: "Terrific. Let me put on the front of my card the time and date of our next appointment. I can see you either Monday or Wednesday of next week (alternate of choice close); which do you prefer?"

If your prospect indicates that he does not want another appointment, you can then start probing again to uncover his concerns and objections. If, on the other hand, he does consent to see you again, you have given yourself another opportunity to close the sale. Use your business card as a sales tool, not merely a give-away.

If you find yourself still not able to close a particular prospect after trying all the tactics and knowledge that we have discussed, it is at this point that you have to realize that some people just can't be sold. Be street smart—don't be discouraged; move on to your next opportunity.

When to Close

Street smart salesmen try to close as early as possible, knowing that more sales opportunities are missed by salesmen who do not realize that their prospect was indeed ready to buy. As a result, many salesmen talk themselves out of the sale by over-selling.

We have already learned that through the use of trial closes, the street smart salesman can test the waters in order to see if his prospect is ready to make a purchase.

The street smart salesman is constantly watching for clues that will indicate that his prospect is ready to buy.

Through observation, a street smart salesman may detect his prospect unconsciously giving a favorable nod of his head. His body may become relaxed, indicating that he has taken the pressure off himself by having made a decision as to what he wants to do. The expressions he makes with his face, a smile or a relaxed forehead, can also indicate to you that he is on your side and is ready to buy.

Street smart salesmen are excellent listeners; they do not want to miss hearing a valuable spoken word that might indicate that their prospect is ready to purchase. Phrases like, "Do you give terms," "How long is your guarantee?" "This suit makes me feel like a million bucks," are strong indications that it is time to go for the close.

Be street smart, listen and observe. As you gain experience, you will have little trouble picking up these invaluable clues that will tell you if it is time to at least try to close the deal.

In summary, the street smart salesman knows that all his sales efforts will have gone for naught unless he is able to get his prospect to commit to purchase. This is the only way he can earn those large commissions—closing, getting the job done!

The street smart salesman constantly closes well because he has studied and developed sales tactics that give him the ammunition to overcome client objections.

As you have learned in this chapter, there is a lot more to closing than just asking for the order. Be street smart—learn as many of these techniques as possible and adapt them to your own situation and personality. Only then will you be able to consistently influence your prospects to make decisions in your favor, which is the bottom line!

The following questions are designed to see if you are starting to think like a street smart closer. See if you have what it takes to get the job done. Read these questions carefully and answer them either in your mind or on a sheet of paper.

1. When you are trying to close a prospect, do you feel you are in control?

2. If not, why not?

3. Do you have a well-planned, thought-out strategy that you can utilize as you get into a closing situation?

4. If not, why not?

5. Do you tend to rely on lowering your price in order to close the sale?

6. If so, why so?

7. How many closes do you have, and what are they?

8. What close would you use to handle each of the following objections made by one of your prospects:
    a) You just have to do better on the price.
    b) There's so much to take into consideration, I'm afraid to make a decision right now.
    c) Everything sounds great; I'll let you know about that money-saving widget next week.
    d) Does this car come in green?
    e) I only wanted to spend $5,000, not $5,500, on my outside deck.

9. Do you utilize trial closes in your presentation?

10. If not, why not?

Now that you have finished reading this chapter, you should realize that street smart salesmen close consistently not because they are lucky; far from it. They close sales because they are prepared. In their bag of selling skills are bundles of closing tactics that enable the street smart salesmen to positively influence their prospects to make decisions to purchase.

After going through these various techniques and still finding that you are uncomfortable closing, selling may not be for you. However, if after studying, practicing, and utilizing these techniques, you have found that your sweaty palms have disappeared, replaced by large commission checks, then you have taken your final step towards becoming a street smart salesman!

Putting It Together

Congratulations, you now know the secrets of the street smart salesman, but don't go out just yet to buy all the toys that you have dreamed about. Knowing the secrets, and putting them all together to use them successfully, are two different things.

Some of these skills may sound easy to you when first read. You may even have said to yourself after reading a chapter, "I knew that." For twenty-plus years, I have seen salesmen fail to reach their potential simply because they knew it all. A few of these skills do look easy when first read. Believe me, they may look easy, but to use them in your world of sales is not easy. It takes practice, it takes commitment, it takes street smart perseverance.

I know, too, many of you will finish reading this page and close this book, saying it was a good book, but nevertheless never implementing the tactics of the street smart salesmen. Others will say that they have seen the light and proceed to carry out many of my ideas for a week or two, and then fall back into their old patterns and habits of becoming a faker, taker, or maker. Don't let this happen to you. You read the book, now give yourself a chance to reach greatness. Don't put it on your book shelf to gather dust.

Because each of us is unique with different strengths and

weaknesses, you must sit down and identify just what your weaknesses are and then use the street smart salesman's tactics to correct the area in which you feel deficient.

After working on your weaknesses, sit down and identify your strengths and again use the street smart salesman's tactics to make your strengths even more effective.

As I said at the end of part one, the individual skills that you have learned are required if you are going to become a street smart salesman; however, you can never get the results that you want until you put them together to run like a perfectly tuned motor.

Take this information and consider it for awhile. Reread those sections that you have to work on, and then go for it!

Success can be yours if you simply do the right thing. The street smart salesman knows this and now so do you. Gain the savvy; and remember, the one who dies with the most toys wins. See you at F.A.O. Schwarz!

P.S.

Just one more thing. After using the principles and tactics in this book, please let me know how they have worked for you. If you have other successful tactics and techniques you would like to share with me, please send your comments to me: Mr. Arthur Rogen, c/o Avery Publishing Group, 120 Old Broadway, Garden City Park, NY 11040.

Bibliography

Carew, Jack. *You'll Never Get No for an Answer.* New York: Simon and Schuster, 1987.

Conklin, Bob. *Egobionics.* New York: Hawthorn Books, 1969.

Delmar, Ken. *Winning Moves.* New York: Warner Books, 1985.

Fenton, Lois, and Edward Olcott. *Dress for Excellence.* New York: Rawson Associates, 1986.

Gayle, Willie. *Seven Seconds to Success in Selling.* Englewood Cliffs, New Jersey: Prentice-Hall, Inc., 1963.

Girard, Joe, and Stanley H. Brown. *How to Sell Anything to Anybody.* New York: Warner Books, 1979.

Goulding, Mary M. and Robert L. *Not to Worry.* New York: William Morrow, 1989.

Handly, Robert. *Anxiety and Panic Attacks.* New York: Rawson Associates, 1985.

Hegarty, Edward J. *Making What You Say Pay Off.* West Nyack, New York: Parker Publishing Co., 1968.

Hopkins, Tom. *How to Master the Art of Selling.* New York: Warner Books, 1982.

Houck, Paul A. *Overcoming Worry and Fear.* Philadelphia, Pennsylvania: Westminster Press, 1975.

Hyatt, Carole. *The Woman's Selling Game.* New York: M. Evans and Company, Inc., 1979.

Johnson, Kerry L. *Subliminal Selling Skills.* New York: Amacom, 1988.

Johnson, Spencer, and Larry Wilson. *The One Minute Salesperson.* New York: William Morrow and Company, Inc., 1984.

Karrass, Gary. *Negotiate to Close.* New York: Simon and Schuster, 1985.

Kirkpatrick, Charles Atkinson. *Salesmanship.* Cincinnati, Ohio: Southwestern Pub. Co., 1971.

Larkein, Alan. *How to Get Control of Your Time and Your Life.* New York: Peter H. Wyden, 1973.

Miller, Julian Asher. *Breaking Through.* New York: Crowell, 1979.

Miller, Robert B., Stephen E. Heiman, and Tad Tuleja. *Conceptual Selling.* Berkeley, California: Miller-Heiman, 1987.

Peters, Thomas, and Robert Waterman Jr. *In Search of Excellence.* New York: Harper & Row, 1982.

Sarnoff, Dorothy, and Gaylen Moore. *Never Be Nervous Again.* New York: Crown Publishers, Inc., 1987.

Seng, Roger W. *The Skills of Selling.* New York: Amacom, 1977.

Sheehan, Don, and John O'Toole. *Becoming a Super Star Seller.* New York: Amacom, 1985.

Siegel, Connie McClung. *Sales—The Fast Track for Women.* New York: Macmillian Publishing Co., Inc., 1982.

Stroh, Thomas F. *Salesmanship.* Homewood, Illinois: Richard D. Irwin, Inc., 1966.

Ziglar, Zig. *Secrets of Closing the Sale.* Old Tappan, New Jersey: Fleming H. Revell Company, 1984.

About the Author

Arthur Rogen has been involved with sales for over twenty years. He began as a sales representative for United States Properties, earning the industry's highest sales performance award. He progressed to Divisional Sales Manager in the company's Eastern Marine Penn Properties division.

After leaving United States Properties, he successfully ran his own real estate development company. Seven years later, Arthur decided to sell off his interests to concentrate on his true love, teaching. For the past twelve years, he has traveled throughout the country as a sales and marketing consultant for companies that wish to develop their sales staff to its highest potential.

Mr. Rogen received his undergraduate degree from Rider College. His graduate work was completed at City College of New York. To obtain more information on the seminars that Mr. Rogen conducts, please write to him care of Avery Publishing Group, 120 Old Broadway, Garden City Park, New York 11040.

Index